Foreword

Firstly, thank you so much for purchasing my book. I appreciate you more than you know.

I have wanted to write this book for a long time and put it off as I didn't have the confidence to be an author.

This changed when I lost another friend to the disease of alcoholism. His name was Sandford, and he was a beautiful soul who always cheered others up and had the best smile in the world.

This book is for you, San, and I know you will be up there gossiping and shining your incredible light on others and probably taking the piss.

The book is meant to be both educational and truthful. I wanted to get an objective perspective out there on how alcoholics think and feel.

I also wanted to let people know that people with addiction problems aren't awful people. They are people who have lost their way in life, people who may have experienced such intense pain they couldn't cope, and self-medication was an option and sometimes their only option.

Trauma affects everybody differently, and you never know what someone else is going through, so please never judge anyone until you have walked a mile in their shoes.

The book highlights some of the life experiences that have shaped my path and the traits of active addiction.

It is sad to say that the stigma around addiction is still experienced every day by millions of people, and we can all do our part to smash that stigma and help our brothers and sisters.

Looking back at my life, I used to wonder whether I was born an alcoholic, and what I mean by that is I was stuck in myself from a very early age, or did I develop alcoholism as a coping mechanism to trauma?

I no longer ask myself and contemplate this as it doesn't matter.

What matters is I found out what is wrong with me, and I took the action and the steps to gain emotional sobriety.

Perhaps you are reading this as you think you may be drinking too much, or maybe a loved one has an addiction, and I pray this gives you some clarity, identification, and, most of all, hope.

I used to attend AA meetings many years ago before finally becoming sober and thinking, nope, that will never happen to me, and sadly, it did.

It's not compulsory to go to the lengths I did to burn life to ashes, but it is vital to go to any lengths to recover.

Here is my story of how I was and what I did to become the woman I am today: happy, accessible, and sober.

This poem I wrote explains alcoholism.

My name is Alcohol, and I have come to rescue you,

You have my word that to you I will always be true,

I will make myself completely available at any time.

Never fear, as from now your soul will be mine

I am excellent when it comes to being a real friend.

My powers are endless, and I will be with you till the end.

You will now be able to feel safe in your skin.

You will be able to breathe easily. I will be your strength within

You will never have to think about your pain.

I will take it and do it over and over again.

I will teach you that you can live without anyone.

It doesn't matter if they all leave and are gone.

That is better for our love to flourish and last.

Be there permanently, and let you forget about your traumatic past.

My name is alcohol, and you now can't live without me.

And now you are going to dare to drop me, let's see.

Now I can turn and show you my true self.

Now I can take away everything, including your wealth.

I will turn you inside out and destroy your soul.

I will remove every person, every dream, and every goal.

My name is alcohol, and I am a cunning foe.

Now I have destroyed you; don't ever let me go.

Nobody Wants to Grow Up to Be an Addict

It was a Thursday morning in February. The rain fell, and everything looked grey, aptly reflecting how I felt inside: empty and soulless. I was desperate, lonely, unloved—no, unlovable—and so very alone.

As I unconsciously stepped off the pavement toward the path of a passing truck, the thought crossed my mind that this could be a way to end the emotional pain I was feeling. It also seemed like a way to recover from drinking—after all, how could I drink if I were dead?
In my warped mind, I believed everyone would be better off without me dragging them down, even my children. The pain of untreated addiction is raw and all-consuming, seeping into every cell of the body. That was all I could think about—every minute sober felt like a stab to the soul. Death didn't scare me; I would have welcomed it with open arms, but I didn't dare go through with it.
What could be worse than death? Death by instalments—that's what. I was looking in a mirror and seeing nothing left of life in your eyes—no hope, just emptiness.

I often see that in people who first come for help. It's a haunting expression, full of sadness and the abandonment of one's soul. The alternative to death was another visit to rehab and all the pain that came with it: endless conversations about why I did what I did, mixed with a bit of expressive dance—

discussions about childhood relationships, diet, sleep, health—blah, blah, blah. The one thing no one ever talked about was why the pain was there and what alcohol gave me that life never did.

I was surrounded by other lost souls, all in the same pit of despair, desperately trying not to make too many waves in the quicksand of addiction. I knew I'd been stuck in that quicksand for decades, and the craziest part was that I wasn't even sure if I wanted to get out. How could I exist without booze? What would life even mean if I didn't have alcohol to look forward to? How would it be bearable? Could I even breathe without it?

Maybe it was fear of dying that day that stopped me from stepping off the curb and ending my miserable existence. So, I stood there, drenched, waiting for my lift to rehab—my second option, my hope that someone could rescue me and physically stop me from screwing up my life even more. I just needed a couple of weeks, and the magic would happen. I would leave rehab a free woman, walking on a trail of rainbows and unicorn farts. The professionals would make me whole again in two weeks, and since I'd paid thousands (borrowed from my dad), it had to work. After all, I was 60% sure I wanted to stop.

If I stopped—or learned to drink like a lady—all my problems would vanish into a rosy horizon. I'd marry the man of my dreams, have no stress or responsibilities, land a job that paid me handsomely for two hours a week, and employers would feel blessed to have me on their payroll.

Welcome to addiction and my insane mind.

Childhood Revisited

The signs that I might grow up with a ticking time bomb in the form of alcohol were evident early on. I was an unusual child—what people often referred to back then as "nervy." Today, I would probably be diagnosed with ADHD and maybe a host of other conditions.

Simply put, I never felt like I fit in—not within my family, school, friends, or even my mind. I had a good childhood—loving parents, holidays, day trips, enough food, and no real hardship. So, I can't blame my behaviours on my upbringing.

I remember sitting in my room for hours, thinking and worrying about things that would never happen. But "probably" doesn't mean "never," so in my mind, it warranted constant worry. I was deeply concerned about a fireball coming from Liverpool to the Wirral and wiping everyone out. I know how crazy this sounds, but at eight years old, I spent many sleepless nights coming up with escape plans in case it happened.

When that fear subsided six months later, it was replaced by a new one: spontaneous combustion. That worry lasted until I was 26, when a work colleague informed me, it was impossible. The relief I felt was indescribable. Another concern was making sure the curtains in my room were perfectly aligned in the centre. I'd ask to go to bed early and stay up late, ensuring the curtains were aligned because if they weren't, all sorts of unimaginable pain would befall my family. I couldn't take that chance.

Nerves ran in the family, so it wasn't surprising that I inherited a large dose. Was I insane? Yes and no.

What I was experiencing was OCD, but back in the early '80s, it wasn't widely recognized, and I didn't see a GP as a child to discuss my fears of combustion, fireballs, and curtain alignment. Maybe my parents knew how odd it would sound and preferred I stay at home rather than be sent to a hospital for those "fecked up" in mind, which I was—fecked and feeling very, very alone.

I spent my childhood fearing the "what ifs"; while my parents tried to rationalize with me, it didn't help. How could they not realize the significance of my concerns? I was, after all, protecting everyone's lives! The anxiety that comes with OCD is crippling and exhausting, made worse by not knowing what was wrong with me or what to do about it. I'll never forget when my dad let me try a tiny sip of his vodka and lime (it was a different time). Although it tasted like lava, I wanted more—no, I *needed* more. Being eight years old, I wasn't allowed more, but I remember how it made me feel—alive. I completely understood why grown-ups drank this stuff. It was liquid heaven. No wonder they all laughed and smiled when they drank—I would too if I had another chance. And eventually, I did.

That feeling of being alive meant that, for the first time, I felt like I belonged in my skin. I could breathe freely, and my heart wasn't pounding out of my chest. Sadly, I rarely felt that way during my childhood—not through anyone's fault but because of a lack of professional understanding and support. This left me trapped in a cycle of doom, day after day.

Deep down, I felt like an outsider to all the good things life had to offer—unworthy, ugly, and ashamed. I thought everything would be okay if I had a better nose and longer hair or George Michael would pick me up from school. I was obsessed with myself—what I was and wasn't. This is what we now call the disease of self, also known as alcoholism. Looking back, I know this period of my life was clouded by OCD and alcoholism. I'll explain more about alcoholism later in the book, but for now, let's say it has very little to do with alcohol, which might come as a surprise to some readers.

A common thread throughout my life is the intense need to help others; this need made my career decisions easy. I wanted to be a nurse, and with that decision at age 17, my mum and nan drove me to Sheffield to begin my nurse training as an adult nurse.

This is where I met the kindest man who sincerely wanted to rescue me, which I never understood back then as I had no idea I wanted or needed a rescue mission.

The Surgeon

In my life and drinking career, many experiences have shaped my future; to name them all would take decades. So, throughout the following chapters, I will summarise the most important and relevant life experiences that shaped my life.

One person who needs mentioning is a man I met as a student nurse.

I used to reflect on this relationship with the usual "what ifs," but I don't feel that way anymore. This one was never right for me; I didn't understand why for many years.

Let's call him Brave Heart (BH) after his Scottish roots and because he was brave to take me on back then.

I met BH when I was a student nurse, and he was a junior doctor. It sounds like the plot of a novel, right? Wrong—because I was involved.

At first, we were just friends. He was a bit of a nerd and posh. BH came from a cultured, classy background. He was intelligent, kind, understanding, generous, sporty, well-balanced—a real catch. And he liked me. I guess my damsel in distress mode was in its early stages at a young age, and I would use this manipulation tactic for decades to come.

On the other hand, I was stumbling through a string of bad relationships and about as cultured as a chimpanzee. BH's friends were as posh as he was, and his family lived in a mansion, complete with a winding road and actual statues. My friends, let's say, were different from his. My parents had taken to living in a static caravan for spring and summer—not an ideal comparison.

That man was always kind to me, always there to listen to my many problems. I would show up at his place in the early hours, drunk and in tears, and he would cuddle me to sleep. With him, I felt safe, a feeling I rarely experienced, so I cherished it.
But there was a big problem: BH wanted more, and I didn't (or couldn't). Why? I thought he was too nerdy, too sensible, and too dull.

On the plus side, he always had alcohol—and not just any alcohol, but posh wines from a wine club—and money. Never one to look a gift horse in the mouth and devoid of morals, I decided I'd give it a go as if I were doing him a Favor. And so, it began. BH brought me flowers and little gifts, and I got to stay at his apartment whenever I wanted, which was far better than my tiny room in the nurse's residence. We had lovely food and fantastic wine—consistently over 14%, just enough to get me wasted most nights—while BH drank responsibly (nerd).

I'll never forget when he paid us for a holiday to Kefalonia. I have beautiful memories of the trip, slightly marred by the fact that I got wasted every afternoon and evening. Looking back, it was becoming clear that I was developing a problem, but I wouldn't admit it for decades.

During the trip, BH suggested that reducing drinking might be a good idea once we returned to the UK, and I agreed. In my mind, though, I was already planning to lie and pretend I hadn't been drinking when I wasn't with him. Sorted.

The relationship was getting serious, which delighted my parents. Finally, Mandy met a good man who would care for her troublesome self, and all would be well.

Because things were getting serious, we were invited to his parents' mansion for New Year's Eve (OMFG). BH reassured me they'd love me and that all his siblings would be there fantastically. Note: They never loved me; they viewed me as what I was: common.

I can't tell you how nervous I was about meeting his mum. I could probably charm his dad, but his mum was another story. She would only want the best for her beloved son, and that wasn't me.
We arrived at lunchtime, and his mum had prepared fillet steak, still practically mooing. Not exactly my idea of lunch, but I ate it politely, even though I wasn't a fan of blood sauce. The house was stunning and incredibly posh, making me feel more on edge. The afternoon was torture. I felt like I was being paraded in front of his family like a lab rat—or maybe that was just my anxiety. I just needed to get through the evening when we could finally go out and get wasted. Yeyyyy.

I've never been one to eat a full meal before drinking (for obvious reasons), but here I was again. We weren't eating in the massive kitchen this time but in the formal dining room. My family's idea of dinner was food served quickly, eaten even faster, and then everyone left. BH's family made dinner an event, with candles, crystalware, and food served in large dishes with silver utensils (Yikes!). Not wanting to overdo it, I politely took about 10 grams of food and claimed I was stuffed, but of course, I accepted a glass of champagne—it would be rude not to.

The alcohol helped, but I was only allowed two tiny glasses. No worries, though; we'd be going out soon, and then I could drink to my heart's content. Hogmanay in Scotland is buzzing, and we had a fantastic time—clouded only by the fact that the police asked me to stop dancing on a grave. BH was understandably disgusted by my behaviour. However, this didn't bother me much, as I figured BH, and the policeman overreacted. What did bother me was his mother, who had been giving me the death stare all day.

I can't blame her for disliking me. I was a mess, with a cig hanging out of my mouth. But she made it evident to me, though never before BH.
I planned to wake up the following day and convince BH that we needed to leave early because I wasn't feeling well. It was the best for everyone—his family didn't need to catch my common ways—germs.

We got back around 3 a.m., and I was starving. While BH went to bed, I raided the fridge and set up a picnic on the floor—no silverware involved, just my fingers and lots of overeating. Then she appeared—his mother—looking down her nose at me and saying, "Classy." I replied, "Thank you," and continued my feast.

The journey home was uncomfortable. It was clear BH was a mummy's boy, and I was an ill-mannered lush. Yet, surprisingly, our relationship grew more assertive.

A few months after the Scotland disaster, we visited Oban, where BH proposed a stunning 3-carat diamond ring. Of course, I said yes—this was my ticket to the high life.

My family was overjoyed, and his family, particularly his mother, was not so much. Plans were made for a castle wedding, and we bought a house together in a great area, along with a cat named Poppy. I had everything I could ever want and was starting my medical science degree. Was this my life?

But there was a considerable problem: me. My drinking was getting worse by the day, and BH was concerned—strangely, I wasn't. I felt like I was drowning in a life I didn't deserve, surrounded by people I didn't fit in with. It made me miserable, and I wanted to run. So, I did.

I went to a work night out and met the girls' dad. Afterward, I returned home and told BH it was over. I was moving out.

BH was devastated, and looking back, I see that my actions were despicable. I broke his heart. BH begged me to stay, saying we could move past my drunken episode, but I was set on self-destruction, so I left. I must have had some morals back then because I signed the house over to him and eventually returned the ring. I must admit, though, that I took a lot of furniture from the house while he was at work for my new apartment with the girls' dad. How I thought that was okay, I'll never know.

Weeks later, drunk, I walked to our old house. BH was away, and I peered through the kitchen window. There was Poppy, sleeping soundly while I sobbed on the floor outside my former sanctuary.

Why did I do it? I felt I had to mess it up because I didn't deserve that life. I thought I was never good enough for him, so I embraced the pain I felt I deserved.

Years later, I learned BH had visited my parents, offering to pay for my apartment because he was worried about me and believed the girls' dad was no good.

I also found out BH married another doctor and had children. From a quick social media gossip, it looks like he's happy—and that's precisely what he deserves: happiness and love.

Note: I bumped into BH once at a hospital reception. It was completely unplanned and a massive shock for both of us. Like a fool, I blurted

out that I'd had a brain aneurysm, then awkwardly said "Hi" about five times. What I wanted to say was, "Sorry." I'm genuinely sorry for the way I acted back then.
If you ever read this, BH, know that you deserve the best in life. I'm so glad you're happy and genuinely sorry for everything.

OCD and me

My OCD has been around for as long as I have. I mentioned it from childhood, and it plagued my existence for many years.
At this stage of my life, I was supported by BH still, and he tried his best to help me with my demons.
I feel it necessary to address what it is briefly, as many people only understand OCD as the need to clean, etc, and it is far more than that.

OCD (obsessive-compulsive disorder) The clinical explanation.

Obsessive-Compulsive Disorder (OCD) is a mental health condition characterized by two main components: obsessions and compulsions.

Obsessions: These are unwanted, intrusive, and distressing thoughts, images, or urges that repeatedly enter a person's mind. Common obsessions include fears of contamination, concerns about harm to oneself or others, and a need for symmetry or order.

Compulsions are repetitive behaviours or mental acts a person feels compelled to perform in response to the obsessions. The purpose of these actions is to reduce the anxiety or distress caused by the obsessions or to prevent a feared event or situation. Common compulsions include excessive cleaning, checking, counting, or arranging objects in a specific way.

OCD can vary in severity, but it often causes significant distress and can interfere with daily life. Treatment typically involves a combination of cognitive-behavioural therapy (CBT), particularly exposure and response prevention (ERP), and sometimes medication, such as selective serotonin reuptake inhibitors (SSRIs).

This definition explains what the illness is, but it doesn't do justice to how crippling it can be. Others say, "Oh, I'm just a bit OCD."

I have briefly covered OCD in the previous chapter, which is about childhood. This chapter centres around the diagnosis that I finally got at age 22 from a psychiatrist.

It always amazes me when people say I'm a little OCD. No, you do not have OCD; you may like things in order.

As mentioned earlier, my nan used to comment how I suffer from nerves and that I would suffer later in life. She was spot on, but not about the diagnosis. OCD had plagued my childhood from around seven years old. My first obsession and compulsion were curtains being correctly aligned; otherwise, my family would be destroyed.

I would spend hours rearranging my curtains in floods of tears as it was exhausting, and the anxiety was horrible and never let up.
I have had so many different symptoms of OCD over the years, and to go through them all would take

an entire book. For this book, the most problematic symptom of my OCD symptoms was intense anxiety. During the years between 18 and 22, my anxiety, panic attacks, and depression had taken over my life, and it was miserable. The only thing that helped was booze, and now I had found the solution, I planned to use it whenever possible.

During this time, BH was as supportive as possible. Still, he was always working or studying, so I spent many evenings alone in our bedroom in the attic, racked with anxiety and, quite honestly, wanting to die. I heard voices and would lay in bed shaking and petrified.

I was taking time off work as I couldn't cope with the anxiety symptoms and awful thoughts that would flood into my mind every damn waking minute. I was paranoid and depressed, and I didn't know why, and my GP had not been any help.
I had been to the GP many times, and he had told me I could be schizophrenic, which was the final nail in my coffin, as this was a condition that scared me to death.

BH made an appointment with a private psychiatrist, and for that, I am eternally grateful, as he diagnosed me with OCD and prescribed the relevant medication. The doctor explained what OCD was and how it showed up. I was so relieved I wasn't schizophrenic, and some medication could help me. I had convinced myself I was insane, my fate was sealed, and I belonged in an asylum rotting.

In those days, there was very little help for OCD, and to be fair, it's probably worse now as the NHS mental health service is on its knees.

BH also helped me pay for a psychologist who I visited for six months, and we talked for hours about coping mechanisms. This lady was retired and charged a nominal amount, which helped me stay alive. I am so grateful to this lady; she was a godsend in many ways.

My drinking had started ramping up to cope with the anxiety, as although it was reducing somewhat, it was still there, and it disappeared entirely with a bottle of expensive red wine from BH's posh wine club.

I would spend time selling the idea of a nice bottle of wine each night with BH, and when he said no, I would change tactics and say let's go to the local as I needed to get out of the house. If BH were working late, often as a junior doctor, I would help myself to a bottle or two of his wine and a few swigs of his posh whiskey from the bottle. BH had started questioning me about my drinking, and I wouldn't say I liked that. This was a feeling that would repeat over and over again throughout my life. If someone complained about my drinking, they had to go from my life as they were controlling. In reality, BH was concerned that I had started self-medicating, and I wouldn't say I liked that.

The OCD was under control to a certain degree, but I had found a better solution, and it did the trick quicker, more effectively, and never failed. Taking a drink meant I didn't have to discuss my feelings for hours or face any problems. The drink had become my new best friend, and it would be faithful for decades to come as a best friend and a toxic crutch for life. I thought this solution was perfectly acceptable as everyone did it, and it was advertised everywhere; plus, I only drank posh wine and drank in bars, so I genuinely didn't see it as a problem—I thought it was an ingenious solution.

Geographics: a move will solve everything.

This period of my life was after I had burnt my life to the ground and left BH.

I was with the kid's dad, and the best part about that is he never judged my drinking as he enjoyed a drink, too.

In the world of addiction, house moves, or a complete geographical change is expected.

As many alcoholics are super impulsive and are no strangers to a removal van, I wasn't the exception to the rule.

I have always been competitive, so why move to the next city when I can move to a tiny island off the coast of Liverpool, The Isle of Man? This island is sometimes known as an island of alcoholics clinging to a rock or where people go to die (retire)
I say this with context to my story only as The Island is stunning, and it is just like going back in time when you could leave your doors unlocked, and there were actual high street shops that were open. The Island is also famous for The TT motorbike races and The Manx Grand Prix, which everyone celebrated with lots of booze. I would fit right in.

I don't know why moving to the island became a plan, but I do know that running away would be an option I would use for decades.

We were on the slow boat to the island for a fresh and clean start: Ian and I, the cat Mia, and my hamster in a red Nissan.

I honestly thought that a move would be the solution to all of my problems, and over there, I would be able to cut down on drinking as it had become a tad troublesome, and I was getting fat. It had nothing to do with cutting down for health, just aesthetics.
Ian and I both had jobs to go to over there and a lovely two-bedroomed apartment (Bliss)
The biggest problem with this move was that I came too, and wherever I went, my alcoholic head came; remarkably, I didn't put 2 and 2 together back then. We lasted six months on the island, and I drank every single day of the change sabbatical and the only thing that changed was that my alcoholism and mental health got worse, much worse.

Back then, I had a million excuses, but as I write from a place of sanity, none were accurate.
On the plus side, Ian and I had decided to get married, and my parents had offered (manipulated) into paying for a honeymoon to The Dominican Republic. At the time, it was cheap as there had been reports of food poisoning. This never concerned me as not many germs can survive on a belly full of 140% rum, and I planned to be very safe from potential food poisoning.

The next part makes me deeply ashamed of my actions back then, but this represents my journey, so I have to tell it like it was and how I thought back then.

Ian's ex would not sign the divorce papers, and we both hated her for this. How dare she rain on my plans? What a bitch, and so we harassed her family. We even sent tons of takeaway food to her parent's address so they would have to pay for it. My insane mind thought it was wrong, and why couldn't she be happy for us? I deeply resented her and her parents with a passion that reflected Satan himself.

In reality, I had taken her husband, her children's dad, her peace of mind, security, and future, and I am sorry for this from the bottom of my heart.
These days, I have a heart, but back then, I think it was mainly pumping alcohol and venom.
I am not saying Ian was innocent, but I can only reflect on my actions back then, as I am responsible for my actions.

I have made my amends to Ian's ex-wife in sobriety, and that woman is one of the most gracious women I have met in my life as she accepted my apology.
If you ever read this, I thank you for accepting my apology. You are more beautiful inside and out than I think you realize, and you deserve the absolute best that life can offer.

I will talk about marriages in other chapters, but for now, we went on our honeymoon and married later. My time on the Island was so dark that deep inside, I regretted leaving BH. I knew that I had hurt him deeply, but I had made my bed and lay in it was all that was left for me. I spent my days working and my evenings and days off drinking.

I remember thinking it would be an excellent idea one evening to call BH as I was running out of money and morals fast, so my heartless plan was to call BH and ask him to give me money as I deserved it. I am unsure why I deserved anything apart from his disdain, but what did I call anyway in an angry rage of self-pity and need?

As you can imagine, he said no, but he was kind to me and suggested I stop drinking. I hear he was showing concern now, but back then, I thought he was mean and holding onto my funds.
An alcoholic will always be very resourceful as the disease has no conscience and has no regard for other people's feelings or circumstances, so I always found the money for booze.

My drink of choice back then was wine (at least 14% or whatever the point) and a unique brew that tasted like death and had a consistency of tar, but it did the trick.

The alcoholic mind is a problem, and due to me continuing my weight loss health kick, I decided an exercise bike in the living room would be a great idea. I had joined Weight Watchers and was allowed a certain number of points per day, so when I ran out of points and two bottles of wine in, I had to jump on the bike and earn more points.
I have the willpower of a champion, so even when trashed, I wanted to keep to my points, so half an hour on the bike was an excellent way to earn myself bottle number 3.

Of course, it never occurred to me that alcohol running through my system and exercise may not be conducive to health, as all I saw was weight loss and sticking to my plan, and it was working.

Ian and I argued daily, and his children never frequented the 2-bedroom apartment we rented because of his children coming to stay.

The TT and Manx Grand Prix came and went, and so did any hopes of cutting down on my drinking, and now Ian had started drinking heavily also. This was one of the main reasons I liked Ian so much, as he "liked a drink" and never said those words as BH did, which I would hear repeatedly throughout my relationships that would mean immediate removal from my life.

"Mandy, don't you think you should cut down?" Whenever I heard those words, I ran as if people had said that to me; they had control issues and didn't deserve a particular spot in my life.

I had one achievement while there: I finished my dissertation and completed my degree. I now was the proud owner of a Bachelor of Medical Science. I will never forget receiving a card from a fellow student with the headline "The World is Your Oyster" and a note to say see you at graduation. I never went to my graduation as I didn't want to be part of it.

Looking back, I know I didn't feel worthy of such an achievement, and maybe it was a mistake. I had

written my dissertation in Drink and didn't remember what my grade was for my degree.
After six months on The Isle of Man, I decided that it was the Island that was responsible for making me drink, and it was due to there not being enough things to do.

For regular drinkers and people, the island was beautiful and offered relaxation, stunning views, and a relaxed atmosphere to thrive. For Mandy, it now appeared to be the ultimate cause for my drinking, and so there was only one thing to do… move…again and leave this god-awful island and never come back.

Note: I applied for my degree certificate in June 2024, and I now have a framed picture of it in my treatment room; the grade is 2:1, which is okay for a dissertation written smashed.

Brain Surgery and the Beast

We jumped forward in time now when I had left the kid's dad, and it was a horrible time.

The insanity continues, and the absolute denial that a problem exists. Most addicts are the best salespeople you will ever meet—they can convince others they don't have a problem, and the most baffling thing is that they convince themselves, too. I would spend hours doing "Am I an Alcoholic?" quizzes online until an internet quiz made it official: I am not an alcoholic, even though I lied in a lot of my answers. The most horrifying thing is I believed my own BS. I also firmly believe that if I had been made to take a lie detector test during my years in active alcoholism, I would have passed around my BS.

I was 31 years old and going through a divorce from my children's father, and as you can imagine, this was an extremely stressful time in my life. I moved out of the marital home with two bags of belongings, a child under each arm, and very little else, but I felt it was the only way to be free and happy. So, off I went to my parent's house (the beer police).

This was stressful, though I am now very grateful to them. Without them, I fear my children may have ended up in the care system. Please don't judge me for this, as I already judged myself and still do, as most addicts do. The urge to drink was so powerful that it often came first, but now I see that I had an illness.

For the mums reading this, I describe the urge to drink as powerful as the urge to push during labour—there is no stopping that force. My daughters are the most essential thing in my life; they are my absolute world and the reason I breathe.

To those without an addiction, it sounds wild that I say this and yet drank, and for years, I hated myself for it because I couldn't understand why I did what I did. Quite honestly, I still can't. This is proof of how powerful addiction can be.

My daughters were around 3 and 4, and I still worked full-time as an operating room nurse. It was hard juggling everything with literally no funds. I began working more overtime to get our place and some furniture, and while living with my parents was stressful, it allowed me to save enough to move out. Interestingly, while I was there, I wasn't allowed to drink, and usually, I was so exhausted that I'd come home, bathe the girls, put them to bed, and crash. I feel I need to note here that during the later years of my drinking career, this wouldn't have been possible, as I drank no matter what, and my willpower was virtually non-existent. Alcoholism never gets better without help, in my experience—it only goes one way, and that's downward.

During this time, I didn't have a monthly period, which I attributed to stress, something my doctor confirmed. However, the doctor did send me for a scan after ruling out pregnancy. I remained on autopilot throughout my days and weeks with one goal: to be successful and a good mum. I so wanted to be a good mum.

This lasted three months before I spent my few free evenings on dating sites, thinking that if I found myself a fantastic partner, everything would fall into place, and I'd be happy. Writing this, all I hear is "me, me, and a bit more me." Writing from a recovered state, with emotional sobriety, I cringe at how I used to be.

I wasn't too bothered about what this man would be like as long as he loved me like I was the only female alive—that would be acceptable. With my bar set incredibly low, I did catch a fish with my "pound shop" net and met Adam (not his real name).
Adam was perfect from the start, in my eyes, back then. He fell in love with me fast, super-fast, and I was with him. This was all utter nonsense, but we will unravel that later.

I mentioned earlier that the alcoholic is a fabulous salesperson, and yep, I sold the idea of Adam to myself as a 5-star package deal when, in fact, he was a 0.1-star "nob." As with any of my new relationships, I could hide my drinking to a large extent, as we would go out and socialize at pubs—everyone drank there, right?

My periods still hadn't returned, so I made my third MRI appointment, as bloodwork and an ultrasound had come back normal.
I had no idea why I was going for an MRI scan, and honestly, it was inconvenient, as I wanted to spend

any free time I had with Adam and my girls. The radiology assistant told me, "You may feel claustrophobic." I hadn't thought I would, but now that he said it, I was sure I would.

The scan wasn't too bad, though it took over an hour as I kept moving. Thinking back, I was shaking because I was withdrawing. This withdrawal was a daily occurrence, yet I never connected the dots. This was another form of intense denial.

Finally, I found a house for me and the girls. This would be our fresh start, our little haven, where we could experience happier times and security. Indeed, once we moved into our house, I wouldn't feel the urge to get wasted every night.

The house was a small, two-up, two-down terraced house, and although it wasn't much to look at, I worked my ass off, and it was ours. I made it home; everything was new for my little family.

The drinking continued every evening. After being forced to abstain at night by my parents, all bets were off—I could drink every night, free from judgment. The girls would go to bed, and the bottle would come out.

In my mind, I wasn't hurting anyone—maybe just myself, but I didn't care about that. I didn't care at all. I viewed my life as follows:
- Kids are taken care of: tick
- Job taken care of: tick
- Bills paid: tick

Vodka then took care of me, and that was a love that could top no other.

Adam would come round a few evenings a week, and life was good—better than good. He surprised me one Christmas morning with an engagement ring. I, of course, said yes, as I would have said yes to anyone with a pulse under 50.

We told my parents, and as the excellent saleswoman I am, I convinced them that it was unrequited pure love (again) this time. I even asked them in front of Adam if they could watch the girls while Adam and I went to celebrate on Boxing Day—using manipulation, a master tactic back then.

That evening, we went into town, and for the first time in a long time, I thought things were looking up. I was getting married (again), he had a job, his own teeth and hair, and he loved me. The evening went well, but toward the night's end, Adam wanted to "show me off" to his friends at a nightclub. I didn't want to go. This was one of the many red flags I would ignore.

Adam stormed off, fuming, and I was left standing in the middle of town, cold, smashed, and quite honestly confused and scared. I had no money; back then, there was no Uber, so I asked a taxi driver to take me home, offering to nip inside and write him a check. To my surprise, he said yes. He must have felt sorry for me.

"Why is this happening?" I whined in the cab. It must be my fault. Adam had started mentioning that I drank too much, which I hated. If I were meant to be controlled, I'd come with a remote control, and I didn't.

Adam arrived in a separate cab, and the cab pulled up to my house. He looked furious. Indoors, I said sorry, not knowing why but thinking it was the best thing to do as damage limitation. I was used to apologizing for everything repeatedly because when you drink like I did, it's unclear if you're right or wrong. Saying sorry was like breathing—essential. Adam started smashing things against the wall, and all I could think was how hard I'd worked to get things for this house. Adam told me I was the "turd on the bottom of his shoe" and that I didn't even compare to his ex. He said my kids were "ming mongs"—to this day, I don't know what a "ming mong" is, but it hurt.

I cleaned up and went to bed, hoping everything would be okay the following day. Adam said sorry, and that was enough for me. He did it because he loved me and was scared of losing me.

How romantic, I thought. Finally, someone loves me for me and doesn't want to change me... much.
We continued our "hallmark" romance, even talking about moving together into his detached house. But deep down, I knew that wouldn't happen. Either he'd become violent, or I would drink him away.
Both turned out to be true.

During this time, I received three letters from the hospital asking me to come for an appointment urgently. Three times, I ignored them. It was inconvenient, and frankly, I didn't care about myself, nor could I afford to take time off work. The fourth letter did the trick—it must have been necessary—so I attended. In truth, my mum ensured I went and came with me to ensure I did.

The appointment was with a consultant who explained that the lack of periods wasn't due to a pituitary tumour but to a brain stem aneurysm, which needed operating sooner rather than later.

My first thought, honestly, was how I was going to drink if I was in the hospital for ten days. Then I asked, "Thanks, doc, but I think I'll leave it."
That wasn't an option. I was informed that leaving it would result in death, and as it turns out, surgery was risky, too—but better than death, so operate they must.

I had to have surgery as soon as possible, so I was booked in for an angiogram a few days later. This procedure involved mapping out the brain's blood vessels.

The night before the angiogram, the girls were in bed at my house, and Adam stayed with me. I had my vodka, so all my anxiety was self-medicated by my old faithful friend, booze. The next part is blurry, but I will explain as best as possible.

Adam had said that I shouldn't be drinking. I insisted I had no problem and needed a drink before the procedure tomorrow. The argument escalated quickly. I tried to go upstairs, but Adam followed me, pushed me down the staircase, and repeatedly banged my head on the stairs, spitting in my face.

These words haunt me, but here goes:
"Drip, drip, drip, Mandy—that's the sound of your aneurysm bleeding. You will die here on the step."
I may have passed out briefly, but I had to come around because the girls were upstairs, and I didn't want to frighten them. Although it hurt, I didn't make a sound.

The following day, Adam told me I had imagined everything, and all was well. But I know I didn't imagine it, and my neighbour later told me she had heard banging. I said it was a picture being hung when, in reality, it was my head.
At the hospital, Adam always played the doting, concerned partner.

The angiogram was scary, and when they mapped out the vessels, it was painful, but it was a means to an end. I guess that end was life if I could call it that. After the procedure, Adam was with me on the ward. I was very anxious, as he could flip at any time and go from zero to demon in seconds. I was the model patient until my femoral artery bled (where they had inserted the cannula). I've seen many patients bleed on the operating table, but this was my blood, and it pulsed out like a red water feature. I quickly lost consciousness.

The NHS was amazing, stopping the bleeding and giving me fast fluids. The next step was brain aneurysm surgery within two weeks. Adam blamed me for the femoral artery rupture, and I agreed—it couldn't have just happened; it had to be my fault. Those days leading up to the surgery were terrifying, so I did what I did best: go back to work with my dark purple/black leg from the femoral artery bleed. I was a master at ignoring problems. I self-medicated every night to the point of blackout. This behaviour continued for many years.

It's just me, the aneurysm, and you, God, today.

My faith today is my absolute rock, but back then, I used God as my fourth emergency hotline
1. Ambulance
2. Fire
3. Police
4. God

If you get me out of this, God, I promise I will change, stop drinking, and look after my body as, to be honest, I don't fancy death quite yet, and I'm not keen on a vegetative state either. Oh, and if possible, can they coil the aneurysm? I don't want my hair shaved off as I like my hair. One more thing, God, I don't fancy an extended hospital stay as I am a busy woman, so let's get this done and me home, and then we can reassess the possibility that I might want to stop drinking. Well, at least on Mondays.
See, I had my priorities right.

Today was the day of the operation, and I was sitting outside the hospital with ten cigs (menthol), so I was slightly healthy. I was underweight, shaking, heart pounding, so scared, and choked while praying to my emergency God.

I had written letters to my girls as the odds weren't great; my house was clean, and the girls were with my parents. I just sat with people, watching how everyone was doing their business, and I was potentially waiting to die.

This was the hospital where I trained to be a nurse and the same theatres where I had seen many patients with brain aneurysms, some successful and others not. I had returned to the operating theatre for a total organ harvest, and I was next in line.
It's interesting how life goes on when someone else's life is falling apart, ending, or beginning, and yet the world continues regardless, like a heartless, inconsiderate narcissist.

After my musings, it was time to go back to the ward, get into my attractive hospital gown, and do this; yep, me and you, God, let's fukin do this.
The nurse asked where I had been as they were ready to take me to the theatre. I had no excuse and could hardly say outside chain-smoking to give the Anaesthetist a challenge, so I just apologized and got on the bed, ready for transfer.

The porter and nurse made conversation, and I was quiet as to why where they were chatting about the weather like that meant anything to me at the moment. I wanted to scream shut up. I'm in deep self-pity right now and feel distracted from my doom. Now comes the good bit, and yes, there is a good bit. This was the most unreal experience of my life.

I was in the anaesthetic room, and my friend Ray, a previous colleague, came in to offer support; he explained that he couldn't be my ODP (operating department practitioner) that day, and I got that if anything went wrong, it's hard to jump into action when your friends on the table.

There was a 2-minute gap where I was alone before the Anaesthetist returned with a nurse.
I can't explain what happened here; all I know is that it was spiritual.
I suddenly felt relaxed and the safest and most loved I have ever felt in my entire life. It was like a whole body and soul embrace of pure love, and strangely, I didn't know if this meant I would live or die. All I knew was that whatever the outcome was, I would be okay, and so would my children.

I know now that this is Jesus, and he always goes before us, and he was with me then as he is today. This was my first spiritual awakening.
When the Anaesthetist returned, I said, "Let to this doc," and we did.

The surgery was a success, and I feel truly blessed to be here today writing this book, as it could have been a very different story.
Note my friend Ray later passed away due to a brain aneurysm and left a wife and two beautiful children. May you rest easy, my friend. You were a ray of sunshine that made everyone's day brighter and a little better.

I promise I will be different now.

There, I was laid in High dependency post-surgery, and waking up, my first action was to check my head, and reassuringly, I still had a full head of hair.
I know how crazy that sounds, but I promised the truth, so here it is.

Second action prayer thank you, God, for pulling my ungrateful ass back yet again, and this time, I will change and be grateful.

I will not dwell on the past.
I will not resent others.
I will not be angry
I will be a better, kinder, and more thoughtful person.
I will be a better mum, daughter, friend and partner.
I never said I would love myself, as even God can't achieve that miracle, but I will live well and maybe exist.

I then opened my eyes and said my date of birth, name, and address. If I could do that, I am not in a vegetative state, and I have my hair, so I would like to return home, please.

Disappointing as it was, this was not an option as I had a catheter and an Arterial line in to monitor my blood pressure, and annoyingly, a nurse would shine a light in my eyes every 10 minutes and ask me questions.

I understand this is necessary and is a procedure, but I was now a total of 24 hours without a drink and in withdrawal, but as I didn't have a problem with drink, I couldn't voice my symptoms. The result was the shakes, sweating, head pain, emotional pain, and confusion, but yes, I am fine absolutely fukin fine. Not only was I withdrawing, but my head hurt, and all I could see was tunnel vision and fuzzy, so like any person with an addiction would do, I asked the nurse to take the pain away.

On a scale of 1 to 10, how bad is the pain?

10, it's 10, it's 10, I said, it wasn't really. It was about a 3, and I've felt much worse, but it could take away some of the withdrawal symptoms, so it was a 10, and at 10, it continued for as long as I could convince the clinicians. It was the only way I could sleep at least and count the hours down until I could drink again, even though I couldn't drink.

Looking back, I am sure they must have known, as it must have taken a horse tranquilizer amount of induction agent to anesthetize me in the first place. They were long ass days and rather unpleasant.

My mum came to see me and even my brother, so it must be wrong as my brother never comes to see me; in fact, I was unsure if he did, but my mum confirmed it, so it must have been true.

Adam was also there playing the doting partner and happily convincing the world he was a real-life saint, and perhaps he was; maybe I had got him wrong, and

it was all down to me and how awful I must be to have a relationship with.
I didn't even want a relationship with me, so why should anyone else, at least anyone who's a good person?

The kids' dad came to visit as he was working in theatres as an agency ODP, and even though he couldn't look after the girls due to being busy while I was in hospital, he could at least come and see me with my other past theatre colleagues.

I was so angry at this and seeing him act concerned, as he wasn't paying maintenance, but I also was aware that getting mad would raise my blood pressure, and I was at high risk for a stroke post-surgery, so I lay there and smiled, taking deep breaths and plotting his demise.

I want to say I spent time evaluating my life and how I could be better, but that would be a lie; I was back in self-pity and needed a drink as it became too painful.

Not physical pain, emotional pain, physical pain I can deal with.

The catheter and Arterial line were out, and that's where I decided to be out, out of the hospital, yes today would be my discharge day why, as I had decided I knew more than the medics and that this was a sane and normal decision to make and so off I went.

I was amazed when the nurse ran down to reception with my tablets advising me to stay, but I seriously did; she did not understand I had to leave as I had had an awful week with brain surgery, etc., and I needed a drink, and I bloody well deserved one.
It is frightening how my well-made life resolutions fall from us so quickly.

I Said NO

I said NO. I know I said no. I said no, right?
This is hard to write but also cathartic, as writing down an event enables growth and freedom when a person is ready. So here goes. This event happened days after I had been released from the dry dock that was the neuro unit.

I was home, and my girls were upstairs sleeping. Yes, of course, I had a bottle of vodka, but it was diluted with lime juice and ice—at my usual ratio of 90% vodka. My justification? I was cutting down, as I took advice from the internet and diluted it with a mixer. In my head, that meant I was adhering to the hospital rules of *no alcohol whatsoever* due to the significant risk of stroke and being on large doses of blood thinners. It was a definitive no-no.

The level of denial here is staggering, but in addition, sanity is lost and replaced with the incomprehensible urge to drink. So, drinking won… again.

Adam was staying at mine to look after me and even made an effort to cook occasionally—how lovely. That night, we had a steak and chips (the only meal he could cook), and I did my usual: 2–3 bites. *Eating's cheating*—that was my motto, and I even laughed about it. The real reason? I was constantly topping up my alcohol intake, and the body of an alcoholic never truly got rid of the last drink. After a few sips, I returned to my usual numb state.

I remember certain parts with a haze and others very clearly, which I guess is a shock and trauma response.

I was lying on the floor, listening to Pink Floyd, and feeling sorry for myself as usual. *No one understands me; why did this happen to me*—that old narrative?
Adam suddenly launched off the settee and grabbed me. I sobered up instantly. The look in his eyes was demonic, and I was terrified. Thoughts of the last attack, where I had banged my head against the stairs, flooded in. My heart pounded, and all I could think was: *My kids are upstairs, I'm on blood thinners—if he does this again, I won't make it*. My kids won't have a mum. My kids will find me dead.

I was in shock, and my body started to shut down. Luckily or unluckily, depending on your view, my body had been here before, so it shut off—but not entirely. *Why didn't it shut down fully when I needed it to?* I remember wearing my favourite red and white polka dot dress, which always made me feel like Pretty Woman. Like her, I was a sex worker (just without pay) but also a *pretty woman* somewhere deep inside. That was my hope—I'd have a happy ending like Julia Roberts one day. Someone would see my pretty woman's side and take me away from everything, including myself.

Adam flipped me over, and I was face down on the rug. It's strange how the brain works because the carpet was all I could think about. *How will I get blood out of the carpet?* Money was tight, and the rug was new—my rug. My girls were upstairs, sleeping. *Shit.* Adam grabbed my pants and pulled them down. I felt utterly helpless. I was severely underweight and couldn't fight back. I had frozen. *It's probably what I deserve*, I thought. *It's just sex. It's best to lie still, get it over with, and return to pretending we're the next Mills and Boon story.*

I said NO. I know I said no. It's imprinted on my brain forever. Even though I said it quietly, not wanting to wake the girls, I said it loud enough and repeatedly enough for him to hear. Adam was possessed. He forced himself up my behind (I still can't know it). I cried into the rug. The pain was intense—pure force and brutality.

I've locked away the next moments deep in my subconscious, but for this book, the next clear memory was telling him to leave now, or I'd call the police. Blood dripped from my behind down my legs, and I did what any person with an addiction would do: I drank.

I also called my friend in Sheffield, who jumped in a taxi and came over immediately. I'll never forget her, even though we've lost touch. She was one of life's rocks, having endured such a tough life, yet she was one of the kindest souls I've ever met. For this book, we'll call her Emma.

Emma was the one who made me call the police. She was also the first to say I had been raped—something I hadn't even realized. If it had been anyone else, I would have immediately said, *of course*, it was rape, but it didn't apply to me. I was insignificant—a drunk. Besides, who would believe me?

The police arrived within five minutes and took me to a medical centre for an examination. The doctor was female, thankfully, and the police treated me with respect. Still, I felt undeserving because I was a fraud. Had I been raped? I was drunk, and though I sobered up quickly during the *alleged* event, I still felt they were overreacting. Maybe they were wasting their time.

The doctor told me there were tears in my anus. Pictures were taken, and my dress—my Pretty Woman dress—was held as evidence, covered in blood. The police dropped me back home, where Emma was waiting. Luckily, the kids had slept through it all. Emma left because I didn't want the kids questioning anything. I'd keep it from them—this wasn't a bedtime story for little girls.

Adam was arrested that night. He denied everything, telling the police I was an alcoholic and insane. But the officer didn't believe him. They wanted me to press charges and assured me they had a strong case for the Crown Prosecution Service.

I never went ahead. How could I? Adam kept contacting me, telling me over and over his version of events—*the real account*. In his account, he was innocent, and I was guilty. In the end, I was so confused, aware that I had recently undergone brain surgery and was self-medicating with alcohol to ease emotional pain. I didn't have the mental strength to go through with a court case. I couldn't keep reliving the event. I didn't know what the truth was anymore.

So, I stored it away in the far corners of my mind, hoping it would never resurface.
What's one more trauma to add to the memory bank?
Besides, vodka hadn't disappointed me in dealing with the past. I was sure my faithful friend would continue to work its magic. All I had to do was get through each day, waiting for the reward that evening brought booze and oblivion.

I informed the police I was dropping the case. The officers were surprisingly disappointed, reiterating that the evidence was solid, and Adam would probably be convicted. But the evidence wasn't enough. My mental state was already fragile. It was my choice—a choice of self-preservation.
Looking back, I wish I could hug Mandy so tightly and tell her she was worthy, was enough, and most of all, loved.

I've included this in the book to acknowledge that it happened. Acknowledgment led to dealing with the trauma and moving on.

My biggest regret

Note that Shaun is my partner; we have a long history of on and off. We are together forever now.

This chapter is about the baby I never got to have. A part of my life will always haunt me, and there isn't a day when I don't think of you, little one.

I was around 35, and at this point in my life, I was still working as an operating room manager in Sheffield. Shaun and I had split up again, and to be fair, I can't even remember why, but I do know that it would have been over something and nothing, and it wouldn't have warranted a breakup.

Shaun and I always broke up, which was not news to anyone. I usually blame him and move on to my next victim.

During this time, my friend had come to visit from home (Merseyside), and we had arranged to go out into town that evening. These were the days when I still enjoyed social occasions, which change as the disease of addiction progresses, and isolation is essential for life and the self-denial of any dependency.

I had very irregular periods, and that is probably due to me being in a constant state of flight, fright, or freeze and the fact that my diet consisted of booze, ready meals, and lots of vitamin tablets.

I looked after myself with copious amounts of vitamins and milk thistle. Milk thistle helps the liver, and although I didn't have a problem with the bottle (lie), I felt it was worthwhile to give my liver a little help. Yet again, my denial in full force would not let me consider that everyday drinkers do not take milk thistle as why would they? The human body is a work of art and doesn't require milk thistle unless you destroy yourself, which I was.

I could not remember the last time I had a period, so I purchased a pregnancy test, which sat in my drawer for a few days until my friend arrived.

I bottled it and never told her until the morning after our night out. It was around 5 am, and we had got home around 2 am, so I was still drunk and decided this would be the perfect time to take the test and confirm that I wasn't pregnant. I couldn't be pregnant as I was on the pill, which I took relatively regularly.

I didn't factor in antibiotics as a risk factor, which, looking back, was so stupid as I was a qualified nurse. I had been prescribed a course of antibiotics for a chest infection, and at that time, I and Shaun were together.

The exact timings of everything are a little fuzzy, but it was all in around eight weeks (the period, the irony) The result did not reassure me in the slightest, as I was indeed pregnant. I immediately ran into my friend in shock about the actual fuk I would do. Shaun and I were not together, and I was already a

single mum to 2 daughters; how could I manage another child alone?
There was only one thing for it: call Sam, and that's what I did, but he wouldn't answer.

One thing many ordinary drinkers/people don't understand about active addiction is that, more often than not, everything is cloudy, and the reasons for breakups and things said in anger aren't readily remembered.

I knew I must have said/done something awful, hence Shaun not answering my call, so I sent a message to say that please reply if it's essential.
This is a message I would send regularly when we broke up, so Shaun didn't understand that this time; it wasn't just because I was sad, bored, lonely, smashed, or in a blackout.

Shaun still didn't call or text, so I texted that I was pregnant and please call urgently.

Shaun finally called. He was on holiday with his son but would return the next day, and we would talk about everything and decide what to do.

I want to clarify a few things here. At that time and point in my drinking career, I could stop drinking for a good enough reason if I tried. It would not be easy, and I would go through withdrawal, but probably without any serious physical harm. I know that later on in my addiction, that would no longer be the case. I couldn't previously stop drinking for surgery or my health (I didn't care or love myself one bit), but I

could regulate to evening/late afternoon only for my children and job.
The withdrawal began while I was waiting for Shaun to return, and we would have 'the talk,' and that was the most extended 24 hours of my life.

Shaun finally returned and remarkably and unexpectedly announced that he would support me completely and, if I wanted, we could have the baby. This was amazing to me, and for once, I would have a perfect family with two parents and not just me battling every damn day.

This time would be different, and I would be the perfect mum, so the journey began; we went to the local chemist and stocked up on pregnancy supplements and lots of healthy food.
This bliss lasted three days until one evening, Shaun came round after work and asked if I needed anything, and as I wasn't drinking and being a role model parent, I said just a kebab, please. (kebabs have salad) I was finding it so hard not to drink, but I had a new beginning now and wasn't going to mess it up again.

That evening was utterly devasting as Shaun turned up with kebab and announced that he couldn't do this and that it would be wrong to stay together just for the baby. Shaun also said I didn't love him, and he knew that, and although I protested my love for him, he didn't believe me.

It took years for me to understand and recognize his decision, and he was right that I didn't love him back then. I couldn't love any man fully without loving myself first.

I stood there in complete shock, and then I did what any average person would (NOT)

I ran outside and scratched his car, and due to not having any available bricks, I resorted to using my kebab to smear over his windscreen.

Shaun left, and I went to the shops for a large bottle of vodka for that would never let me down and has been a faithful friend up to now. The emotional pain inside me was excruciating, and vodka made it bearable and disappear.

The next day, I took a day off work sick, and Shaun texted to say he would pay for a termination.

I have always been against abortion, and at the time, I couldn't imagine that I might have to think about having a termination myself. I needed help and plan to have this baby and somehow cope financially, emotionally, and physically.

It's not the best idea to have a baby when you have had previous aneurysm surgery and are a raving alcy, but I would forego booze if needed to have my baby. I asked my parents if they would look after child number 3 while I continued working.

My parents had co-parented with me since the girls were toddlers; they had also watched my demise into alcohol addiction and how I became more and more lost in my life, which was chaotic. I completely understand their reasons why they could not do this again as their lives had already been put on hold due to caring for the girls while I worked or had manipulated them to have them more for other reasons based around self, myself me, me and me. I needed a plan, but where could I go, and what could I do?

I needed to continue working as I couldn't keep the house and a home for my girls, and Shaun wasn't an option.

The biggest reason was booze, and I am deeply ashamed of writing this. I couldn't stop drinking and had drunk every evening since Shaun announced he couldn't do it.

I did the unthinkable and booked into a termination clinic; Shaun had dropped the money off as I went private due to me being only around six weeks pregnant, and waiting for The NHS may have taken months.

I was taken to the appointment by a friend, and that day, I was completely numb and heartbroken; here I was having a termination, so I guess I am pure evil after all.

Shaun was calling all morning and begging me not to go through with it, but how could I trust him as he would probably change his mind again? Life has taught me not to trust men or anyone, not really. Note I do trust these days again, but back then, I had doom-coloured glasses, and I wore them as a permanent fixture for self-preservation.

The actual surgical procedure was painful, as I insisted; I did not want painkillers as I wanted to feel everything as a sort of self-punishment.

The tablet termination was not an option due to having a previous brain aneurysm.

The words from the doctor as she finished the procedure will haunt me, 'all done' like I had just had my hair blow-dried. I had to stay in the clinic for a couple of hours on a comfy reclining chair with around ten other women. We were offered painkillers, and I refused as I was evil and had just murdered my child, so stop being nice to me ffs. I left the clinic, and yep, I got smashed and, for good measure, stoned.

I regret having a termination, and the guilt I felt and still feel is crushing.

Addiction is all-consuming, and making huge life decisions in a state of emotional torture is nearly impossible. I made the wrong decision that day, and for that, I am sorry.

Sam and I often talk about this, and we both handled it like children ourselves, and our pain and trauma clouded our decisions.

I am comforted by my faith these days and know that I will meet my baby again one day, and until then, they are being loved in heaven.

I loved you, little one, and I am sorry I couldn't love myself enough to bring you into the world and give you the life you deserved.

Back Surgery

I was 36 years immature.

I may have had a problem, but not with alcohol—at least, not yet. This period of my life, I have revolved around work, my children, plenty of potential suitors, and plenty of drinks.

I was now the proud owner of the title "Medical Sales Representative" and was finally earning good money. I had a company car—a white sports Audi A3 with bucket seats and tinted windows. I drove it like a maniac, which quickly earned me a speeding ticket (three points) and a burnt-out clutch. Both are under 1,000 miles—impressive, right? My manager didn't think so.

On the plus side, I hadn't been caught drinking because I never drank and drove. I never drank in the morning either, but I'm pretty sure that if I'd been breathalysed, I would've been over the limit. The body of an alcoholic takes longer to process alcohol, but we'll get to that later in the book.

Often, I was up and out by 5 am to attend surgeries. I could have swum the English Channel using only my earlobes if I was under the legal limit.

Things were looking up for me. I had money in the bank for the first time, not just an overdraft. I owned a three-bedroom semi-detached house with a large garden. My ducks were in a row, and I wouldn't let anyone—or anything—stop me.
Until I stopped myself again.

As a medical sales representative, I drove hundreds of miles a week. Even though my car had been fixed, with the burnt clutch displayed in the company's reception area (lovely), I started experiencing pain in my left leg. I've always had a high pain threshold—part of the territory of being a stubborn fool—but this pain was different. Sometimes, it made me nauseous. Still, I soldiered on because I was needed in theatre and couldn't let anything hinder my world domination.

I didn't go to the GP because I was afraid that if my suspicion were confirmed—a herniated disc—I'd need to go to the hospital. And frankly, the selection of drinks available to inpatients wasn't worth it. This pain persisted for months, growing worse by the day. My self-medication increased accordingly (for pain relief, of course). I got better at hiding it, but one day, I couldn't. I was assisting in surgery at my local hospital when I suddenly felt terrible. My back twinged—no, it stabbed as if a hot poker had been jammed into it. I also had that awful water-in-the-mouth sensation that meant vomit was imminent. I made excuses and hobbled to the restroom, locked myself in a cubicle, and put my head between my knees to give myself a stern talking-to. I needed to get back to the theatre. As I was leaving the restroom, the nurse in charge stopped me. "Mandy, you look awful. You're grey," she said.

For the record, I was a bit grey and sweating profusely, but I would have returned to the surgery if she had let me. Instead, she made me lie down with my legs elevated in the staff room. I thought she was

overreacting at the time, but looking back, I'm grateful. There are some fantastic clinicians in the NHS, especially in operating theatres.
So, you'd think I rushed to the doctor or A&E. Nope, not me. I went home around 4 pm and, you guessed it, had a drink—or twelve.

Three weeks later, I admitted to maybe having a tiny back problem. It wasn't the pain or the numbness spreading to both legs and my bottom that prompted this confession; it was because people at work were starting to notice. That was my nightmare.
After a national sales meeting, I tripped over my foot because I couldn't lift my left one. A colleague informed me that I needed to see a doctor that day or he'd tell my manager.

I begrudgingly took his advice and made an appointment—several weeks later.

The GP immediately arranged a scan and a specialist referral. To my surprise, he also asked about my drinking again. This pissed me off because I'd told him countless times that I only drank 14 units. He didn't believe me clearly, which was odd because *I* thought me.

Side note: Alcohol can contribute to back problems, though that wasn't the case here (or so I thought). While alcohol abuse doesn't directly cause a slipped disc, it can lead to nutritional deficiencies, muscle weakness, impaired coordination, and bone deterioration, all of which increase the risk of spinal injury.

Since I'm "special," my scan was scheduled for the following week. Of course, I wasn't unique—I was just in a high-risk category for paralysis. But "special" sounded better, so I believed my own BS again. From my brain aneurysm days, I was no stranger to MRI and CT scanners. As with the aneurysm, it took ages due to my twitching (withdrawal).

The following week, I met with the neurosurgeon, Mr. Jellinek. Yes, that's his real name, and no, it's not a joke. He's an incredible surgeon; I'd worked with him in theatre before. I was relieved to have such a skilled doctor handling my case.

Mr. J asked how I'd managed the pain. Naturally, I couldn't be honest and say, "Well, I couldn't waste valuable drinking time as an inpatient, could I?" So, I just told him it wasn't that bad. He looked at me in disbelief and said I'd been lucky, but the disc needed to come out immediately.

Lucky? Seriously? Wasn't a brain aneurysm terrible enough? But I had a choice: paralysis or a short hospital stay. So, surgery it was—after all, I needed my legs for work.

The surgery was scheduled for the next day, which, as luck would have it, was at 5 pm—right during my usual drinking hour. By the time I arrived at the hospital, I was already in withdrawal.
I remember thinking, *I hope it doesn't take a horse dose of anaesthesia to knock me out.* Thankfully, I was underweight, so that wasn't a concern. (People with

addictions often require more anaesthesia than others.)
As the saying goes, I had bigger fish to fry, but I'm being honest about my thoughts.
I remember laughing myself to sleep—a defence mechanism I'd picked up along my trauma-filled journey—and it helped me cope.

Once again, I believe God gave me another chance. The operation was a success, though Mr. J reiterated how lucky I'd been. I hate being lectured—it's condescending and boring (I was such a dick). That evening, when I returned to the ward with my spine intact, I was in complete withdrawal. So, naturally, I claimed my pain was unbearable to get morphine. But the morphine didn't help because the pain wasn't in my back.

The real pain was from withdrawal and my thoughts. What non-alcoholics don't understand is that, for alcoholics, drinking is medicine. It numbs feelings and thoughts—an incredibly effective survival tool. I spent the entire night sweating, staring at the ceiling, counting the hours until I could leave.
In hindsight, maybe I should have brought a bottle with me, but only an alcoholic would do that—and I wasn't one. Honestly, the level of denial here is frightening but sadly true.

Mr. J discharged me the next day, and I went home with strong painkillers for my now-mild pain. The pain was 100 times better than in the past few months.

Since I wasn't an alcoholic, I waited until 3 pm to have a drink. I paired it with painkillers to ensure utter oblivion—after all, I'd had a tough few days. *Note*: I know a woman who has since recovered, but during her addiction, she left the hospital one Friday evening to drink a bottle of wine at a local pub. She even bought a couple of gin and tonic cans to enjoy while watching TV in the hospital. This woman was utterly shocked when the nurse told her she couldn't sit in the ward drinking.

Denial is like a set of blinkers on a horse.

Looking back now, I can see how crazy my actions were. But I write truthfully about how I thought and felt during my many years of alcohol addiction and dependence.

Husband number 2: a marriage of manipulation and pain.

We will call him MF to offer some anonymity.
I met MF when I left nursing to pursue my career in medical sales. I was around 37, and my drinking career was in almost full bloom. I drank every single night and some afternoons when appropriate (BBQ or social event)

I was a single mum and had an array of failed relationships behind me and one common denominator of relationship doom: me. I, of course, never blamed myself for my view; I was unlucky in love and very unlucky at that.

During this period, I met a group of female friends I went out drinking with, and we also spent time together as the three amigos as we were all single mums. We supported each other with childcare and the difficulties of being a single mum.

I loved my new job as a sales representative for an orthopaedic company, and although a steep learning curve, I excelled, and I was a great sales biatch which was a surprise to all, including myself. In later years, I would realize many people with an addiction are masters at sales and manipulation, and I had a complete toolkit.

I had more money than I ever had and some spare cash to go out drinking with my new friends, so I did that regularly.

I met MF on a very drunk Saturday night in town. MF was over 6 feet and stocky, which back then was my type. I wanted someone with caveman traits who would sweep me off my feet and look after me and the girls, and maybe then I would be able to reduce my drinking.

I asked MF if he would like to take me for a meal, and he asked when, and my reply was now. It was midnight, and I was starving as I hadn't eaten all day, so I didn't hinder my drinking. MF laughed and agreed, so we went to an Indian restaurant. MF wore a suit jacket, jeans, and good shoes, so in my mind, he must be wealthy, and if so, I would go home with him that evening.

I can only imagine how classy I must have looked eating the curry as once smashed, it was always like feeding time at the zoo, and I am sure this time was no different. MF bought two bottles of wine, which I happily drank, and I am sure the conversation was utter bollox but also fascinating as ever as I always told my best tales drunk….not.

After the meal, we went back to his, and disappointingly, he lived in an ex-council house with two bedrooms, and worse still, it wasn't his; it was a rental. At this point, I would have gone home with Hitler, so here I was, shitfaced and crashed out with my legs open and my dress above my waist (class). I am not sure if he carried me to bed, but I woke up around 7 am, had well-regulated consciousness, and had just come on my period. I asked MF to go to the shop and get me some sanitary wear, and to his credit, he did.

Looking back, most decent men would have run a mile, but MF had an idea that he would be the one to save this unfortunate woman, and all she needed was love and direction; how wrong he was.

A common trait of alcoholics is that we move fast in a relationship, so the next day, I decided to have a barbeque at my house and invite everyone.
I am writing this with a sane mind now, and while writing, it's astonishing how I thought this was normal, but I genuinely did. I thought I had met the love of my life...again and had to move quickly so no one else could get my prize and future happiness.
The BBQ went well; everyone, including my parents, friends, and kids, liked MF. I had a big summer house, and all of the kids put on a play, and we all watched a mini theatre production of pissed adults watching their children perform.

I know how bad this sounds and why my parents would even agree. Still, you have to understand that I had a full tool bag of manipulative tools and sold the idea to everyone that this was the best plan ever and that my future happiness depended on it. I also sold the idea to myself that MF was the answer to my prayers. MF would be a perfect dad to my girls and a supportive, caring, and loving partner.
After that evening, MF moved in, and a few months later, he moved in officially.

My ducks were in a row. Finally, I had an exciting future, and to top it off, MF suggested we get a dog to complete our family, so we took a trip to the local animal shelter and got Sam.

Sam was a tri-coloured border collie and the best dog ever. He was crackers, naughty, and quirky, but most of all, Sam was loving, and he has been my rock throughout my sobriety.

I believe Sam was a gift from God as he helped me and the girls every day of his life and was a beacon of hope and love in some dark times. They say the dog spelled backward is God, and I saw love in his eyes every day, even when I was unlovable.
Sam passed on the 25th of 2024 at age 14-17. He had been my boy for 13.5 years, and I know we will be reunited one day. Sam was the campest dog you could ever meet, and I know he will be up there in heaven mincing with other dogs and eating everything he shouldn't. I miss you, Sambo, every day, and you are always in my heart.

I was still drinking every night, and MF liked a drink too, and that made everything more perfect as he wouldn't nag me about my drinking. This would change in later years, but for now, all was well. My career was taking off, and I won an award for being the best salesperson of the year.

Whenever everything is going well, I can always self-sabotage, and that's what I did. Around three months before meeting MF, I had been having an affair with a very senior colleague at the company. My morals back then were non-existent, but now I had met my future husband; I didn't continue the affair with said colleague, well, almost.

I had to attend a work event with senior work colleagues and a surgeon to discuss an idea for a piece of equipment. The senior man was attending and had asked to go for a drink before the central meeting to discuss why our affair had to end. I explained why, and he wasn't taking no for an answer and was angry. Certain people aren't used to hearing no, so he made it uncomfortable during the meeting. The meeting ended, and we returned to my room to continue chatting; by then, I was smashed and slept with him one last time. I regretted this the following day and felt ashamed and guilty as there was MF at home minding my children while I was out sleeping with another man.

I returned home that afternoon, and MF had some exciting news that made me feel like Satan himself: he had booked a holiday for the 4 of us to Lanzarote. I had a decision to make: do I tell MF about my unfaithful night, or do I forget it and pretend it never happened as it was over and wouldn't happen again? I took counsel from my friends, who advised keeping the dirty secret as it would be useless to come clean. One thing about me is that I am great at keeping everyone else's secrets, but I have always found it hard to keep my own. This one was killing me, and I had to tell MF precisely what happened and take my chances.

The best option would be to confess in Lanzarote as he couldn't run away there, and I would have more chances to speak my way out of this on holiday. I plucked up the courage on night three while inebriated (Dutch courage). MF went crazy and reacted like any average person would when they had spent their time and money on someone and had it thrown back in their face with betrayal. I ran off and sat behind the hotel complex with the stray cats for a couple of hours until I needed the bathroom. MF was still fuming on my return and went out, so I passed out.

The following morning, MF said he would try and sleep with me, and if it felt ok, we could put this behind us as he thought I was manipulated, and I didn't have a clue if I had been or not. I was relieved there was still a chance of a future with him, so we slept together.

On reflection, this is toxic, but my mind was in bits for years, so the unacceptable becomes acceptable regularly.

The kids slept through the commotion and knew nothing about any of this and, so the following evening, was over the moon when MF proposed in a Chinese restaurant, and I said yes; little did I know how high the stakes were and how guilty I would be made to feel for the years to come.

The holiday ended, and when we got home, MF began to plan the wedding at warp speed, which I thought was odd but went along with it as I was in no position not to.

MF made me feel safe, which I longed for and needed, so I met with MF and his friends even on my own. That evening ended in a brawl in a restaurant, and MF and his son fought with a group of men because they were mouthy. I was secretly proud. I mean, what a hero my man was.
The wedding was uneventful; it was at the Barnsley registry office with a bit of a do at a local venue. My dad had hired a limousine for me and the girls (bridesmaids), which was an event in itself. When it pulled up, I asked if it came with an MOT as it was ancient, and Kojak was my driver.

We ended the night at a local pub, and my friend went away looking for a venue that did karaoke. I was a fantastic singer on a skinful (not). MF called me after 30 seconds, saying, "Where is my wife?". This was a sign of things to come, as during the marriage, MF never trusted me, and even though I didn't cheat again, I can't blame him. The marriage should never have happened, and my knight in shining armour turned out to be a toad, and I was no princess.
During our marriage, it became more and more evident certain members of his family thought I was a loser, especially his posh sister and his niece, and forever looked down their noses at me. This always confused me as although, yes, I drank too much, I was hardly a terrible person and tried my best every day to make a decent, loving wife.

I know now that I could never have loved anyone, not properly anyway, as I didn't love myself, I didn't even know myself, and I didn't know why I was intent on destroying myself through drink.

The marriage lasted six years, and the last year was terrible. MF became the beer police, and I spent every day trying to convince him that I could drink that evening. The arguments were a daily occurrence, and the atmosphere in the home was toxic.

MF became resentful and angry, and I grew more and more depressed. I would be put on a booze ban and would manage a few days occasionally, followed by even more drinking and more tension. MF began to be controlling, and I could cope with that, but he also tried controlling the kids, especially my eldest daughter, who had her problems at the time.

All I needed to do was cut down on my drinking, and yet I wouldn't say I liked MF for constantly nagging and lecturing me on how I had a drinking problem. The cycle continued round and round day after day with the same promises to stop and the same failure. There was only one thing for it: a house move as a new start would do the trick.

No, and yet I thought it might be just the solution. We moved into a detached 4-bedroomed property, but as with any geographical sobriety move, it didn't work. Why?

I came too, as did my alcoholism in bucket loads.

I will never forget one evening when my parents came to visit, and I had gone to bed drunk. My mum was in the spare room reading, and MF was conversing with my dad, which was more of a heated debate. They were debating on my current condition as a potential alcoholic, and this resulted in a shouting match.

MF was shouting, "She's an alcoholic," and my dad was denying this and saying that I just drank too much. Both were correct, even though neither of them knew what an alcoholic was.
This is the unfortunate fact about alcoholism: ignorance.

I include myself in this ignorance as I, like many others, thought alcoholics drank in the morning and were unsavoury characters drinking out of bottles and on the streets.

The result of 6 years of marriage and many failed attempts to control my drinking and be a good wife ended in divorce. This was my second divorce and my 100th failed relationship, but of course, I didn't see any of these unfortunate circumstances as my fault; it was just bad luck.

I moved on quickly as this was the only way I coped with the desperate loneliness of untreated alcoholism to a new man who ticked all the boxes for the moment.

One thing that prevented happiness was that I missed MF and wanted him back in my life, or so I thought. I went out on a mission to get him back and succeeded on the condition I cut right down on my drinking and proved to him I was not an alcoholic. I would prove to him and his posh sister that I can do this. I have beaten a brain aneurysm and many other life challenges so that I could do this one thing, but I couldn't.

I would sneak bottles into the house and hide them in the garage. I would pretend I was doing laundry and drink out of the vodka bottle every day. The bottles would be found, and sometimes, I would forget where I had hidden them. This was so painful as vodka had become my elixir for life and the only way I could breathe. I couldn't stop as it was too damn painful, so I manipulated as much as possible to drink, and if all else failed, I would lie and drink anyway.

It wasn't that I was being awful or that I didn't care for MF and my children; I had lost the power to choose whether I drank or not. The worst part of it is I had no idea of this loss of power and just thought I was an awful crap person and deserved nothing but pain. These thoughts made it acceptable to stomach the fact that I was being emotionally abused every day, as I thought I was not worth anything better.

The battles continued until MF gave an ultimatum: it was him or the booze, and I told him to shut the door on his way out, and that's precisely what he did. The final chapter in our relationship is so demoralizing I wanted to die.

It had been three months since MF had left for the final time, and my eldest was angry at me for drinking, and we had a big argument. My daughter called MF, and he told her to come through to his and stay there for a few days to let things settle down, and that's what she did.

At this point, I thought about what a fantastic father he was and how kind he was to offer help in that way after everything I had done. That evening, after a bottle of vodka, I turned up at his door where my eldest was upstairs asleep and never knew any of the following.

I missed MF, and I knew I had messed up again, but surely, this time, I would make him realize that I did want to stop drinking and be a family. I walked straight into his living room and noticed a Christmas card on the mantelpiece from a woman. I ripped it in two and continued my best sales pitch for my return to his girlfriend's place.

MF listened and said he would always love me, and I took this as good news as this meant my sales pitch was working, but I needed to step it up a bit as he seemed to like this new woman on the scene.
It was after midnight, so we went to bed and had sex; it wasn't making live; it wasn't makeup sex. It was cold and distant. MF treated me like I was nothing, and I felt like it.

I left at 5 am as I didn't want my eldest to see me there. MF clarified that we would never get back together, that last night was a mistake, and that he

was falling for the new woman in his life. I begged him to reconsider as I sobbed uncontrollably on the floor, and he looked at me as if I was shit on his shoe and an absolute nobody, unlovable and pathetic.
I have never felt so low and alone as I did on that morning. I thought I was lower than low, and if someone had offered me an escape route from life, I would have grabbed it.
I did the only thing I knew what to do to take this pain away, and that was drink.
After that event, my alcoholism switched up to its final notch of total self-destruction.

Germany and Career Suicide

This event is etched in my brain forever; at age 43, I experienced the most shameful experience of my life—or so I thought. That sentence alone is a testament to how alcoholism's final three letters describe the insane mind. It wasn't the abuse, the loss of relationships, or even the loss of my soul. No, it was this event that highlighted my state of mind in the final two years of active alcoholism.

I was functioning to some degree but still working because it kept me from going off the rails. I had worked with a large medical device company, selling unique products that could restore patients' quality of life. A previous senior colleague who believed in me had supported me in getting the role, even though I didn't know why, as my confidence was at an all-time low.

The role was a fantastic opportunity to make lots of money and do something I had always wanted: help others. The first two months were spent training and covering radiology cases for a procedure to reduce patients' pain and shrink cancerous growths in the back area. I loved it. Despite having to travel hundreds of miles each week, it was worth it. I had fantastic colleagues and a great product, and for the first time, I desperately wanted to get sober.

I didn't aim for complete sobriety—just a reasonable level, not the recommended 14 units a week, which I thought was unrealistic. My goal was to drink only on the weekend and avoid alcohol at work functions or sales meetings. But the plan failed; I still drank every day. I'm not sure why I thought I could prevent drinking at sales events, but I believed my lies and went off to my first sales meeting with the company and career I loved.

The meeting was global, meaning all senior colleagues would attend. I was excited—and scared. Monday morning, I drove to Manchester Airport in my beautiful, brand-new company car, feeling like my life was finally coming together. But it was early morning, and I was twitchy. I knew that if the police stopped me, I'd probably be over the limit, having drunk copious amounts the day before.

I drove carefully, heart pounding, constantly scanning for police cars. I just needed to get to the airport and park the car, and everything would be fine. Somehow, divine intervention or pure luck saved me from ever being breathalysed or hurting anyone while driving, something I deeply regret and am not proud of.
I arrived in Germany, and the national sales meeting began. The day was inspiring and motivational. We discussed new products that would significantly improve patients' quality and longevity of life. I felt blessed to be part of this and promised myself I wouldn't ruin the opportunity by drinking.

One presentation was given by the main boss, a friend of my boss, Robert, who had helped me get the job. As he spoke, my alcoholic mind drifted, imagining myself up there next year, blowing everyone away with how much success I'd achieved and how many new accounts I'd brought to the company. It's a common trait in untreated addiction to dream big—prominent. Like many in addiction, I had a huge ego.

After day one, we all went to an upscale restaurant for dinner. With about 300 colleagues attending, I needed to be on my best behaviour. Robert couldn't participate and had given me strict instructions to act like a professional. I looked respectable in my blouse and black trousers, even wearing heels. The problem? Alcohol was everywhere, and everyone was partaking. It seemed rude not to join the celebration, so I did—and kept going until I was utterly wasted.

In my drunken state, I talked loudly over everyone else, convinced my stories were fascinating and that I could help them succeed with my unique insights. I noticed the main boss looking disgusted at my behaviour, but I rationalized that it was because he couldn't hear me from so far away. I figured I'd talk to him the next day.

The following day, I couldn't remember everything from the night before, but I knew I had to behave today. At breakfast, people were frosty, but I had yet to be asked to leave. If I could redeem myself today, I'd be fine. Throughout the day, I made small talk, blaming my intoxication on feeling unwell and not having eaten much. My colleagues seemed to buy it, so I vowed to be a professional that night.

That evening, the company had hired a boat for dinner and a mini-cruise as a thank-you for everyone's hard work. I tried to skip the event but was strongly encouraged to attend. As soon as I boarded the boat, my "I won't drink tonight" mantra dissolved when the waiter offered champagne. Before long, I was trashed again.

The rest of the night was hazy. The disco started, and everyone was having fun—except the main boss, who sat with two senior colleagues. For some reason, I felt it was my duty to get him to join. I asked his assistant, who agreed it would be a great idea. But the boss didn't share our enthusiasm. He told me to leave them alone, and one of the men stood up, asking me to leave immediately.

The next thing I remember is sobbing and banging on the boat's captain's compartment window. Somehow, they let me in, offered me a bottle of wine (which I drank straight from the bottle), and even allowed me to use the boat's tannoy system for an impromptu guided tour—though I'd never been to Germany before and had no idea what I was saying. The following day, the shame hit me hard. At breakfast, everyone was silent, staring at me. I quickly ate alone and returned to my room to pack. I just needed to get through the final day and go home. But a director sat beside me on the coach to the office and made small talk. I thought this meant I wasn't in trouble, but I was wrong.

When we arrived, the director escorted me to the boss's office, where he, two other directors, and his assistant were waiting. The assistant couldn't even look at me. I apologized, though I couldn't remember everything. The boss appreciated my apology but said they had felt threatened. I had two choices: be fired and face a tribunal or leave voluntarily with a payout.

I was in shock. I should have told them I had a problem with alcohol and needed help, but I couldn't admit it—not to them and not to myself. I chose option two, left the company, and sobbed at home. The next day, I convinced myself it wasn't my fault and called several no-win-no-fee legal firms. But none thought I had a case. Looking back, I know I was responsible for my actions but also highly unwell. That afternoon, I drowned the pain in a bottle of vodka and wrote a plan to cut down on drinking, believing I could hide this incident from future employers by simply leaving it off my CV.

Note: In a rebellious act, I told them they couldn't have the car back for a month, as it was parked in my garage. I was furious they hadn't helped me when I was mentally unwell.

My many attempts at relationships.

From the age of 14, I longed to be in a loving relationship with someone who would take the emotional pain I felt away and save me.
I only understood many years later what or who I needed saving from. I had loving parents, and no childhood is perfect. We all make mistakes as parents, but mine tried their best, and I knew I was loved.
I know now that I was running away from the only person I couldn't run away from, myself, although I tried and failed for decades.

I thought that if I could find Mr Right, I would be happy and that I could put all of my energy into making that relationship perfect.

From a young age, I planned to be the perfect wife, mum, and all-round unique human being. I would draw pictures of my white house, complete with the picket fence.

One thing most people don't realize about alcoholics is willpower; most have a bucket load, and I was no exception. I was determined to make this life happen, and my quest to find the perfect partner was on, and time was ticking.

There are so many relationships to mention in one book, and I won't go into everyone in detail as it's the

same pattern that has been repeated over four decades. I will give an example and show that this happened on a cycle over and over again throughout my adult life.
The relationships I have mentioned have significantly affected my life, and each one has made me the person I am today.

As I write, I understand more and more that I have never had a type as many people do. The one thing I wanted was love and for the pain to stop.

This is how many of the relationships began.
The digital age was a godsend for me as I was like a kid in a sweet shop and dating sites, and there are loads of them. I would set up my profile and paint myself a fabulous superwoman who kissed a lot of frogs, popped some good pics on a tag headline, and waited for the magic. There were no filter pics back then, so I always note that I look better in person and am not very photogenic.

This was how I met my partner Shaun 15 years ago, who reminded me of my tagline on that particular site. "I am not bad looking but find it hard to relax," which meant I come in a pretty package, but I am a flaming nightmare, and I drink to oblivion regularly.
I would send my chosen prey a message and strike up a conversation, and hey presto, a relationship is incoming.

In active addiction, the behaviour of an alcoholic can be selfish, and I was ticking a lot of boxes on that front. I would listen intently to the new man's stories, see what he liked and didn't like, and then become the perfect partner.

If he liked climbing, I was a climber, movies, I am a moviegoer, etc.
The biggest thing for me was he must like a drink, and by that, I mean he must drink like a fish and never, and I mean never, bring up my drinking.
I became the perfect potential wife for the new unsuspecting partner and had multiple engagements. The relationships would last anything from 3 weeks to a few years, and then I would burn them to the ground and move on to the next victim.

I am ashamed of my behaviour and the multiple hurts I have caused other souls who didn't deserve such venom and pain. At the time, I couldn't see what I was doing was wrong as I only thought about myself and my happiness, so they were casualties in my war against myself. I honestly thought I was just unlucky in love.

The real reason was that I couldn't love as I didn't love myself. I was consumed in self and emotional torture, and as we know, hurt people hurt people.
I went around like a roaring lion, destroying any man who dared to love me. I always had the old excuse of ending a relationship because he became controlling, i.e., he was concerned about me killing myself through booze. I couldn't see this or understand it, and it would take years of recovery to know the truth of my actions and a painful wake-up call of how much of a toxic person I was and many amends.

I used relationships like ordinary people use therapy to feel better, and this was the case with Shaun, my real partner, in every way. Shaun had always seen through my BS and knew how fuked up I was even when I couldn't see it. We have continued our on-off relationship for many years, and now, in recovery and sane, we are together for good.

It is funny how life works sometimes and that a soulmate can show you the parts of you that need work and healing. Shaun had some issues of his own to work out from his dad leaving when he was a child, and four years ago, in recovery, I mentioned he always ran away. I am an expert in running, so I know what I am talking about.

Shaun and I had two years apart while he got some therapy and worked on his demons, and we came back together finally and for keeps this time. Relationships aren't easy, and I don't envy anyone who lives with an alcoholic, active, or recovered as we think and act differently from an average person. I can still be a selfish asshole, but at least these days, I can see it and remedy it. I can accept and see when I am being unreasonable, and we talk regularly and move along with life.

In the end, it has been a happy ending, and we have a house, and although it hasn't got a picket fence, we are so glad, and I feel loved and safe. I am entirely faithful and filled with gratitude that I am settled and in a loving relationship, and the Biggy is I love Shaun wholly and genuinely, as these days I know how to do that.

The "I want out"

This event occurred during my final months of active alcoholism, and looking back, I was not of sound mind. However, I would never have admitted that to anyone.

All that I knew was that I was in so much emotional pain and turmoil that it was getting harder and harder to function daily.

I was still working full-time but doing the bare minimum to get by under the radar.
At this point in my drinking career, I knew that I may have been ever so slightly drink-dependent but still vehemently denying I was an alcoholic.
Alcoholics don't work full-time and do not have a mortgage.

It was a weekday, and things at home were fraught. My eldest was getting worse with her mental health issues, and she was also at an age now (around 15) where she was seeing me for who I was: a drunk.
It was around 4 pm, and I finished work for the day and did my workout in the garage attached to the house.

I worked out daily and still took copious amounts of vitamins and milk thistle, and this is all part of the self-denial that I was healthy and not an alcoholic. Workout done

House cleaned
Work done
Drink time
To cut down, I decided to drink Malibu and one vodka as I had read online that this could help cut down.

In complete denial, I would drink from the Malibu bottle, and those slugs wouldn't count as they were not drunk from a glass.

I would follow up with 1-2 massive vodkas with lime. I would always finish the 1-litre bottle of Malibu before coming out of the garage after my workout. On this particular day, my eldest was waiting for me, angry, disillusioned, and upset.

On reflection, I completely understand why she felt this way; after all, she needed me at that point in her life, and although I was there physically, I was not emotionally.

My daughter wouldn't let it drop, and she wouldn't let it go. Why did I drink? I am a useless and unfit mother.

I always think that the truth hurts the most, which hurts me to the core, for deep down, I knew the truth, and the truth is she was right, and I am guilty; I didn't understand what at that point.

I ran upstairs and locked the bedroom door. She was banging on the door and screaming and wouldn't stop, and neither would the pain. It was too much,

and as an alcoholic, I didn't/couldn't handle pain, so
I had to make it stop and go away somehow.
I went to the ensuite and took every tablet in there
(mainly codeine)
My daughter broke the door and called an
ambulance.

I sat on the floor crying and just wanted the pain to
stop.
The crying continued in the ambulance, and I
sobbed. I asked the paramedics to please drop me off
as I didn't want to go to the hospital and have that on
my record. They were kind and patient but refused,
so I went to casualty. They asked me why I had taken
the tablets, and for the first time, I was utterly baffled
as I didn't know why, and it would be nice to know
why.

Unfortunately, the NHS isn't equipped to deal with
the massive problem of poor mental health and
addictions, so I was left alone in a cubicle for hours.
They did blood and an ECG, and I waited and
waited.

I felt hazy, sick, sweaty, and alone, so at 3 am, I went
home and walked out of the department.
It was not the best plan as my phone was dead and I
had 20 pence in my purse, so I walked home for 3
hours.

On my walk, there was a group of men, and one
whistled at me. I wasn't scared at all. I was angry, and
in so much emotional torture, I picked up a large
stick, and I wanted them to attack. In my mind,

perhaps if they beat me up, at least I would feel something that had to be better than the numb nothing inside of me.
The men walked away, and I continued walking home.

It was early morning when I got home, and my friend had stayed to look after the girls, who were still asleep. I thanked my friend and went to bed for an hour before the girls got up.

That ended the situation; I wasn't offered support or help. I was to be judged by the medical team who looked after my eldest, and most of all, I would judge myself as the worst mum ever.

I talked to the girls about why I did this and how sorry I am that they had to witness it. At the time, I couldn't explain why, as all I could feel was either emotional pain or numbness.

To a regular/heavy drinker, that would have been enough of a devastating experience to stop, but for me, how could I stop it was the only remedy I knew to stop the pain.

It dashed hopes and dreams that pissed all over my attempts to drink responsibly.

I feel it's only fair to add here that the following services, books, and professionals aren't useless for the heavy drinker, but for the real alcoholic, they are as helpful as a chocolate fireguard from a fiery inferno (just saying).

I will begin with the most obscure Chinese medicinal herbs.

I remember many years ago taking my children to Meadowhall (a giant shopping centre in Sheffield) and taking them on the train for an adventure. This was a big mistake, as keeping your eyes and ears open with two toddlers is no mean feat.

There is a reason they say you need eyes in the back of your head.

When we arrived at Meadowhall, the bickering was in full swing, and you have millions of nerves in your body, and this day, every one of them was raw and activated.

I was always exhausted, and that day was no different.

After my girls had a cake in hand and down their dresses, we walked around the shops. My youngest was a magpie and regularly snatched anything shiny; this day was no exception. She only grabbed one earring, which was disappointing as she could have gotten the other to make a matching pair. (just being honest)

It was close to late afternoon, and I was getting twitchy for my usual routine of tea, bath, and bed for the girls, not me; I remember eating's cheating.
At that point, we walked past a Chinese medicine shop, and I didn't know why I thought it was a good idea to walk in and ask for help, but that's what I did. My alcohol dependence could be cured there and then; how amazing. They listened for around 30 seconds, and that was good enough for me as I didn't really believe I had a problem, so they potentially diagnosed my future alcohol addiction problems perfectly.

To pay for this miracle cure, I had to use my overdraft, which was nothing new, and as it's super expensive, it must be good, right?

Wrong, it tasted like camel dung, and I took it to the letter of instruction and washed it down with vodka to taste away as neat vodka tastes dreamy.

I also thought it didn't work as I had taken it on a stressful day, so it wasn't the medicine or my lack of willpower. It was purely lousy timing.

I, of course, wasn't to blame. It must have been a faulty batch.

Self-help books.

Most of the people I have helped and know who struggle with addiction have a full complement of self-help books.

They are usually written by someone who has never faced addiction personally and has an academic background.

I will not mention them all, but I read approximately 15 and often used them as a coaster for my drink.
I also read in the evening while in a blackout, so that was the problem. You see, it was just a damn timing issue.

Self-help books can be practical for regular drinkers to cut down, but if I were a regular drinker, why would I be reading how to cut down on alcohol? Every drinker doesn't do that. They decide to stop, and guess what? They stop.

Unfortunately, I didn't see the irony here.

Relationships.

I used relationships regularly over the years as, indeed, a good man would make me safe, happy, and content, therefore not needing to drink.
It was just happiness and loneliness that made me get smashed every night.
I will talk more about relationships in other chapters, but for now, know that I honestly believed that a new relationship would be a 100% cure for my drinking. It was not my fault I drank. It was just circumstances.

I lived for dating sites where I could get a new man in minutes, and not only that, I could pick. This online dating was my remedy for denial as, like a kid in a sweetshop, I chose the next yummy option and devoured it in the desperate hope that he would save me.

It was years later I realized that this was an impossible task as I was not only in denial, but I also dumped them the second they mentioned cutting down or stopping my relationship with my most enormous love (booze) and going on to the next. This cycle continued repeatedly, yet I never linked the fact that the common denominator of the failed relationships was me.

Who knew?

Sadly, not me.

Geographical cures

In a previous chapter, I talked about the Isle of Man; however, below are the places I moved to for a magic cure for my drinking, even though I didn't have a problem.

Wales, Birmingham, Barnsley x 4 houses.
I genuinely thought I was drinking, as I wouldn't say I liked the house or area I lived in.
The level of denial here is astounding and yet is expected in the world that is addiction.

It's so much easier to blame someone or something else for using a beloved crutch than to accept defeat, and I am no quitter.

I have moved 19 times, and each time was a fresh new start that turned into the same old nightmare.

Doctor

My GP never helped me. Why is this?
I was never honest and wanted a cure to my unknown ailments quickly and effectively without actually having to stop drinking or take any responsibility.

Self-denial and self-deception can and do lead to death, and sadly, I have been a witness to this fact with lost, beautiful souls who are no longer with us. I would visit my GP around three times a year as I just knew something was missing from me emotionally, and I felt alone, confused, and exhausted. The exhaustion was constant, so I had blood tests, which would always come back normal. I remember the doctor would ask how many units of alcohol you drank, and I would always reply 14 as he never asked how many units you drank before 5 pm. In my insane mind, I never drank more than 14 units before 5 pm, therefore telling the truth.
Because I never told the gods truth, my GP never helped me; how could he?

This never stopped me from blaming him for not listening to me and the things I never said.

I guess what I wanted was a psychic GP who would diagnose my problem without me knowing and miraculously solve it without me giving up my beloved vodka.

Psychologists and counselling.

Tick and tick to both. I quite liked the sessions as I got to sit on my soap box and was lyrical about how awful my life was and that they would drink too if they had my life.

I blamed everyone, including my family members, and the best part was they listened, passed me tissues, and most of all, they fell for every single word (lie) that came out of my mouth; how awesome.
This cemented that I was an unfortunate soul and victim, giving me the green light to self-medicate my way through the following decade with a gold star for effort and deception.

I remember a few years ago, someone said to me, "How do you know if an active alcoholic is lying? They are speaking." Oh yes, I can relate to that, and alarmingly, I believed my version of colourful and factual events yet again.

This was a skill I used to manipulate others as much as possible for my gain over and over again while not realizing what I was doing or what effect it would have on others, and quite frankly, back then, I didn't care.

I was in so much emotional pain I did what I had to do to survive, not live, survive.

I am not saying that these professionals are not effective in treating people with addictions. What I am saying is the alcoholic can be the number 1 nominee for a Grammy award in acting, and I played the part of the victim like an A-lister.

Beer police (my parents)

This is a further part of the book I do not relish writing about, and although I have made my heartfelt amends to my mum and dad, I am still ashamed of my behaviours.

My parents tried everything to help me; they looked after my girls and me throughout my life, and I see now how utterly heartbreaking it must have been for them to watch their only daughter be swallowed up into addiction.

My mum often came to stay at my house to help me cut down; she suggested gardening, days out, walks, chats, cooking, etc.

Each late afternoon, I would have my acceptable glass of wine in front of my mum, who would congratulate me and reassure me how well I was doing. I went to bed early with my secret stash of vodka.

In my mind, I resented her, for although I knew I might not be drinking to the recommended limits, I was hardly an alcoholic; I mean, come on.

This happens all over the world in millions of families where the addicted one's parents and friends do everything in their power to help their loved one. I guess I am coming with the truth here and my experience of the many alcoholics I have worked with. It is not that the addicted ones don't care or love their families and friends; they do. The guilt eats away at them; worse is that they can't understand why they continue the fee.

I have an event etched in my mind that I am deeply ashamed of, but bringing the complete account of addiction here is what I promised to do, warts and all.
I had been working all day in the operating theatres, and I can't say that this day was awful or different from any other day. The day was as usual at work, and as usual, I was speeding home safely, knowing I had half a bottle of vodka and an entire bottle of wine in the fridge. I had 20 menthol Superkings, and my plan was like any other day: to sit by the window, drink, and smoke to oblivion.

My mum put a massive spanner in my plans; she had looked after the girls all day as usual when I was working; she had bathed them, read them a story, and were fast asleep.

I walked into the house and went straight to the fridge, where there was no wine.

I asked her where the wine was, and she said she was trying to help me. I didn't need it, so she walked towards the door and up the path.

I knew that half a bottle of vodka would not do the trick of intoxication, and I wanted, needed the

Wine.

I followed my mum up the path and threateningly made her tell me where it was.
As I write this, I am in tears as this feels like a different me. Back then, I must have looked possessed and scared as my mum shook and quickly got into her car.

Mum, I'm so sorry and love you very much; you and Dad have been the best parents to me and my children.

Drug and alcohol services

I enlisted the help of Barnsley alcohol and drug addiction services in my final years of active alcoholism.

It was pretty cool that the initials spelled BADAS, and in my crazy, insane mind, it was a compliment as I was badass.

Again, I will add here that this service may work for the heavy drinker, and I have minimal experience with drugs apart from perhaps recreational in my younger years.

Looking back, it's a little fuzzy that those last years of drinking all kind of rolled into one long, dark period. I do remember them asking how much I drank, and even though I was more truthful with them than my GP, I still lied.

I said I had one bottle of wine a night and a few vodkas (authentic), as they never asked me how big the vodkas were.

We discussed my triggers at length, and I learned something that made me realize I had lots and lots of triggers. I think daylight and the moon may have also been a trigger.

Again, for me, it was therapeutic to sit and tell a stranger how shit my life was, and again, the tissues came out.

I was drinking due to stress, and although I agreed wholeheartedly, I never gave a thought to why ordinary people don't have to drink themselves into a stupor every time they experience stress.
They were the professionals, after all, and if they say I'm drinking because of stress, I will go with that, as it takes all responsibility off my shoulders, result. To help me with this stress, they gave me an Indian head massage; however, this was at 5 pm, so I couldn't enjoy it as the treatment encroached on my drinking time, which was inconsiderate of them.

My homework was to fill in a drink diary, which, like a good student, I did, and I stated proudly that I had only been having two drinks a night. This was a truth.

I had managed to have only two glasses a night, and on my last meeting with BADAS, they said Well done, and I am on the road to recovery.
I never did tell them that the two drinks were pint glasses, and the drink was 40% proof, but a win is a win.

If my attempts to stop/regulate are unusual, I can tell you they are not.

The self-denial of addiction can be fatal, and many do unfortunately lose their lives.

One final memoir that illustrates this denial.
A few years ago, I visited a man with active alcohol addiction in a hospital aged 46 with cirrhosis to try and help him when he left the hospital.
His words to me, "Mandy, whisper, I don't want people to think I am an alcoholic."
This man passed away four months later and never did get the miracle of sobriety as he couldn't be honest to his innermost self.

Rehab 1

The day I arrived, I entered a residential rehabilitation unit in Runcorn, UK. It was early November 2017, and I had finally admitted that I, Mandy, had a huge problem with alcohol. I had lost control of my drinking and needed help.

How did I know I had a problem and was probably an alcoholic? The consensus was out, and even though I usually say opinions are like assholes—everyone has one—this time, not everyone around me could be wrong. Deep down, I clung to the slim hope that I wasn't a person with alcoholism and that I was going to rehab to learn how to drink responsibly, to prove I wasn't an alcoholic after all. This demonstrates the insanity of active addiction, and I was the queen of ignorance when it came to alcohol.

I had arranged for my girls to be looked after, and as always, I ensured my affairs were in order before any trip. Affairs means work, housework, food shopping, and paying bills upfront. Standing outside the rehab facility, I thought: *What if someone sees my company car and reports me to my employer?* I immediately started mentally planning how I would handle that imaginary situation. It's safe to say my biggest worry was people finding out what a lush I was when my concern should have been: *What will this week look and feel like without booze?*

I grabbed my bag, locked the car, and knocked on the rehab door. I felt nervous but mostly deflated. *How had it come to this?* It was never on my bucket list to go to rehab and spend thousands of pounds I didn't have staying in Runcorn with a bunch of alcoholics and drug addicts. *Had I made a mistake? Had I exaggerated my drinking problem?*

The door was answered quickly, which stopped my spiralling thoughts. A friendly lady with about five teeth greeted me and took me to the counsellor who would admit me. This wasn't what I had expected. The place was expensive, and the greeter wasn't exactly five-star service. *Admit me? What is this, an asylum?* On reflection, the lady with five teeth was a recovered addict and one of the kindest souls I would ever meet. She had been clean and sober for years, while I couldn't even manage 24 hours. Oh, the ego can be an absolute superstar.

The admission process was thorough, and for the first time, I told the truth about my drinking. For once, I wasn't judged, and that felt refreshing. The process included a Skype call with a doctor from their sister facility in Bradford for a Librium prescription. Librium is often prescribed for alcohol dependency to reduce withdrawal symptoms and the risk of seizures. At first, I thought they were overreacting—didn't they know I was a nurse and a successful saleswoman? This wasn't an overreaction. I had been to the funerals of people who died from going cold turkey.

Alcohol dependence can be so severe that the body seizes when alcohol is abruptly stopped. A medical detox is not only recommended—it's essential to avoid death.

After being admitted, I was given a buddy, Carry, who showed me around and introduced me to my two roommates, Sarah and Sam. My little room had a single bed and a copy of a 12-step program's text on the bedside table. Sarah had struggled with addiction for years, and Sam's alcohol addiction had left her with organ damage—she had been a paramedic. I felt like a fraud; my problem wasn't as bad as theirs, right?

The fact that I had suffered a brain aneurysm, abuse, back surgery, multiple failed attempts at controlling my addiction, failed relationships and marriages, and that my mental health was hanging by a thread didn't seem to register. Over the years, I learned that addiction spares no one—regardless of social class or profession. Both Sarah and Sam were kind, compassionate people, like most addicts, who had turned to drugs or alcohol to self-medicate their emotional wounds caused by trauma.

At lunchtime, Carry took me to the dining room, which looked like a greasy spoon trucker café with the same menu. Other inmates were serving a full English breakfast, and I sat down at the last empty chair next to a glamorous woman named Mandy. Mandy would become a friend in the months that followed. She was one of those people who could light up a room with her smile and humour.

(Note: Mandy passed away a year later, losing her battle with alcohol addiction. She called me the night she died, but I was too drunk to answer. She left a voicemail—silence, with background noise. Mandy fell and passed away, leaving a broken family. She desperately needed help beyond what rehab could offer.)

Back to day one. The canteen was noisy with chatter and laughter. I couldn't eat much as I felt sick, but as I left two sausages on my plate, a fork darted over and speared them, making me laugh. It's incredible how appetites return after a period of not poisoning the body.

After lunch, I took my first dose of Librium and returned to my room to sleep until dinner. I felt safe there, in the bubble of rehab, where the outside world couldn't touch me. Carry took me to dinner, and again, there was laughter and conversations about other people's journeys and how they were finding the facility. I had only booked a week, as that's all I could afford, and besides, I thought that would be enough. *I wasn't a real alcoholic, was I?*

That night, we all sat in the smokers' shelter and talked about everything and anything. Those evenings were filled with laughter and tears as people shared their heart-wrenching pasts. Some of the most accurate, raw, and unique people I would ever meet were there. I was amazed by how those in addiction could still smile and help another soul despite the traumas they had endured.

During my seven days, I followed the same routine: roll call every morning (thoughtfully), medication with strict monitoring, and meals scheduled like clockwork. The group attended daily sessions on the 12 steps to recovery, though I couldn't join the evening fellowship meetings due to my medical detox. That suited me fine—I could read my AA book and sleep. I read the entire book, thinking it was ancient and irrelevant. Six months later, it would become my lifeline, but at the time, it was just a coaster for my wine at home.

Some moments stand out vividly. One was a group exercise class for expressive dance. I've never laughed so much as we, a group of rattling addicts and drunks, learned dance moves. I now realize people in addiction know how to laugh and have fun. We forgot why we self-medicated for that hour and lived entirely in the moment.

Another memory was November 5th, when we were outside watching fireworks. A group of youths stood outside the gates, mocking us "saddos" in rehab, leaving a half-full vodka bottle as a temptation. This is the ignorance that surrounds addiction. People don't understand that those in rehab are desperate for help—none of us planned to end up here. The phrase "be kind" is popular, but genuine kindness is understanding that addiction is not a choice.

On day five, some inmates received family visits. I watched a single mum battling addiction greet her young daughter with so much love. People often think mums in addiction are selfish and terrible parents. In my experience, many are struggling with demons, battling immense trauma. These mothers love their children more than life itself and often feel shame and confusion about their drug use. Addiction is an illness, not a choice.

That same evening, a young man in the facility had an emotional breakdown. He had suffered years of abuse and coped by using drugs. Sadly, he lost his battle with addiction shortly after leaving rehab. His family had begged for help, but there were few treatment options, and the pain became too much to bear. He passed away in his early twenties, another sensitive and wounded soul lost to addiction.

On my final day, we walked in a local park. We looked like a group of ordinary people, fully clothed, washed, and fed. But the looks of disapproval from passersby were everywhere. People took their children away from us as if we had an infectious disease. Society often sees addiction as a shameful condition, blaming people with an addiction as weak-willed or a drain. In my experience, most addicts are driven, determined individuals who have unresolved trauma. We need to treat the pain, not just the symptoms.

On my last day, a counsellor told me I needed more time in rehab, as I would drink again. He said my ego was massive. No one asked why I was hurting or what drinking gave me that life didn't. I couldn't afford more time and felt on top of the world, ready to face life.

I returned home and attended a few 12-step fellowship meetings, but soon decided I didn't need them. I thought I had mastered alcohol. I stayed sober for three weeks until I convinced myself I had overreacted. An alcoholic wouldn't be able to go three weeks without drinking. Wrong. One Friday night, I bought a bottle of vodka, planning to save it for Saturday. I drank the lot that Saturday and didn't have another sober day until February 2018.

(Note: An average drinker doesn't go to rehab, but in my mind of denial, I pushed that fact far away. Yet a tiny doubt lingered. I knew I was done for.)

I Have a Choice

I could never understand why I repeated the same actions for many years. It was as if my life was on endless repeat, and no matter what I did, it always ended with the same scenario: me feeling sorry for myself, wallowing in self-pity after yet another failed relationship, job, friendship, house move, etc.

I had a choice, right? Theoretically, I could exert my power to choose and decide not to drink, which would be mission accomplished. But if it were that simple, why hadn't I considered exercising my choice and saying, "No thank you, I don't want a drink because I tend to end up in trouble," or something to that effect?

To this day, it amazes me when people say to those who are addicted, "Why don't you just stop?" As if I'd never thought of that before! Thank you so much for your helpful and insightful advice; I'll follow it until I die and be forever in your debt.

Every single addict has tried, over and over, to stop. They've spent years analysing why they can't, feeling awful and like a failure as they continue to relapse. Alcohol is a cunning foe, which is why so many addicts don't understand why they keep "choosing" the substance over their loved ones and their lives.

I remember a lady who was previously in active alcoholism once asked me, "Do you have a choice?" It was during rehab, and while still on Librium, I answered, full of ego, "Erm, yeah, of course I do."

This moment changed my life, and my ego was shattered. She asked me to put up both hands. In my right hand, I was told to imagine everything I loved and held dear to my heart. This was easy: my daughters, my dog, and my parents. Then she held up my left hand and said, "Now imagine in this hand, you have your bottle of alcohol (vodka)."

If I had the power to choose, what would I choose?

I stared at this woman, thinking, "Is this some sort of sick trick, or is this Librium playing with my already fragile mind?" "Erm, my right hand, of course—my kids, etc."

The lady replied, "And what's been happening?"

A jaw-dropping moment for me. I didn't have the power to choose—I had lost the power to choose. This loss had occurred repeatedly in my life, regardless of the consequences.

That evening, I refused to come out of my room and sobbed all night. How had this happened? When did I lose the power to choose? And more importantly, what happens now?

Now, I did have a choice. I had two:

Continue as I had been and return to the pit of alcoholism and more insanity (I should add here that my sanity was hanging by a tiny thread).

Get help and admit that I am Mandy, and yes, I am an alcoholic.

The Silent Echoes – Trauma and the Path to Alcoholism

Introduction

Trauma, in its many forms, leaves lasting imprints on the human psyche. For many, these scars do not heal on their own, leading to profound emotional pain and vulnerability. To cope with overwhelming distress, some turn to alcohol as an anaesthetic, seeking refuge from their inner turmoil. This was certainly the case for me, and the ironic thing is I caused so much of my trauma, and the worse things got, the more I tried to self-medicate the pain away.

This chapter explores the complex relationship between trauma and alcoholism, unravelling the reasons why trauma survivors often become vulnerable to substance abuse and addiction.

Defining Trauma

Trauma is an emotional and psychological response to profoundly distressing or disturbing experiences. It can be acute (a single overwhelming event), chronic (repeated exposure to stressful events), or complex (long-term exposure to traumatic circumstances, often starting in childhood). Trauma reshapes how individuals perceive themselves and the world, distorting their emotional regulation and coping abilities. Common examples include:

- Childhood abuse (physical, emotional, sexual)
- Domestic violence

- Military combat
- Loss of a loved one or sudden life-altering events
- Neglect, abandonment, or betrayal
- Sexual assault or intimate partner violence

In my experience through working with others in addiction and from my recovery, trauma doesn't have to be serving in Afghanistan or horrendous abuse. Many people don't even realize they have suffered trauma, and it has been hidden deeply in their subconscious mind.

I know I have suffered traumatic events in my life, but I can't recall which event made me the way I was back then and what made me turn to alcohol to ease the pain. As I think back, maybe it was OCD and the anxiety I felt, or perhaps it was my inherent need to self-destruct from being a young child.

I guess it doesn't matter what came first, the old chicken and egg analogy; what matters is I drank decades of my life away to replace something that was missing, and that something is peace of mind, and I lacked that in a big way.

Our subconscious minds are super powerful and do a fantastic job of protecting us from pain, so we bury experiences and traumatic events under "do not disturb." In my experience, we need to disturb and wake them up to process events and heal. I had to do this to find inner peace and true freedom.

Alcohol as a Coping Mechanism

For trauma survivors, alcohol often becomes a tool for emotional regulation. The numbing effect of alcohol can temporarily dull feelings of shame, guilt, anger, and fear. In the short term, it may relieve intrusive memories or flashbacks, allowing individuals to escape their emotions.

Alcohol provides the magic elixir to suppress anxiety and numb life.

In my drinking career, drinking would help me celebrate and commiserate, whichever was needed that day. Drink never let me down and was a helpful friend on every occasion. Alcohol became my solution to life.

The one thing I didn't expect was it dumped me. The relief from alcohol stopped working; it stopped taking the pain away. The relief it gave me had disappeared, and the only thing that remained was pain and a very destructive cycle.

Alcohol alters the brain's chemistry, acting on neurotransmitters like dopamine and serotonin. These "feel-good" chemicals offer temporary feelings of euphoria or relaxation.

Alcohol had become my saviour, my god, and my life. However, my tolerance built, and I was entirely dependent. I required more alcohol to achieve the same relief, and the only relief it gave me in the final years was loss of consciousness but no emotional pain relief.

Alcohol had stopped helping me in my attempts to cope with trauma and gradually morphed into a destructive addiction.

This is often referred to as the jumping-off point. How did that look for me?

I couldn't live with or without alcohol.

Trauma and the Brain: A Cycle of Pain

To understand the link between trauma and alcoholism, it is essential to explore how trauma impacts brain functioning. Traumatic experiences disrupt the brain's ability to process emotions and regulate stress responses. The amygdala, responsible for fear and emotional regulation, becomes overactive, triggering intense reactions to perceived threats, even in safe environments. At the same time, the prefrontal cortex—responsible for decision-making and impulse control—loses effectiveness, making it challenging to manage urges or make rational choices.

Alcohol initially soothes this hyperarousal by dampening the nervous system, creating a temporary sense of calm. However, repeated alcohol use further dysregulates these systems, weakening emotional resilience and deepening the trauma-alcohol dependency cycle.

This is an insidious process, and unfortunately, for many potential alcoholics out there, this becomes a statistic. I have seen many people cross that invisible line from everyday drinkers to alcohol dependent and never return. This can often lead to the gates of hell, and I know as I was a frequent visitor.

Post-Traumatic Stress Disorder (PTSD) and Alcoholism

A significant number of trauma survivors, especially those diagnosed with Post-Traumatic Stress Disorder

(PTSD), are at a heightened risk for alcoholism. PTSD manifests as intrusive memories, nightmares, hypervigilance, and emotional numbness. For those with PTSD, alcohol serves as a means to reduce hyperarousal, helping to suppress re-experiencing symptoms or numbing emotional pain.

Studies show that individuals with PTSD are significantly more likely to develop alcohol dependence than those without the disorder. Alcoholism may provide temporary relief but intensifies the disorder in the long run, leading to severe mental health deterioration.

In my experience, trauma is subjective, and we are all different in how we respond to external events. What may be traumatic for one person may be a breeze for another, but trauma is trauma regardless of its origin, and if you feel it, it's a genuine feeling. As trauma is subjective, the need to self-medicate the pain away can be a genuine requirement to live.

Childhood Trauma and Alcoholism: A Profound Connection

Childhood trauma has been identified as one of the most significant risk factors for developing alcohol dependence later in life. The Adverse Childhood Experiences (ACEs) study revealed that individuals exposed to multiple forms of childhood trauma are exponentially more likely to struggle with addiction.

Children exposed to trauma may grow up in environments of instability, neglect, and emotional pain. Without the support or tools to process their trauma, they often carry the unresolved pain into adulthood. This leaves them vulnerable to seeking out maladaptive coping mechanisms like alcohol, which offers momentary relief from the deep-seated distress that originated in childhood.

Childhood trauma does not have to be physical or even emotional abuse. It can be something you weren't even aware of then and has been buried in the subconscious mind.

A wounded inner child can present itself in many ways, and addiction rears its ugly head as a toxic relief aid again and again.

Numbing Emotional Pain

- **Unresolved Trauma**: Addiction often stems from the desire to numb the deep emotional wounds carried by the inner child. Suppose a person experiences neglect, abuse, or emotional abandonment in childhood. In that case, they may turn to substances like alcohol, drugs, or food to escape the overwhelming feelings of sadness, fear, or anger.
- **Temporary Relief**: The wounded inner child uses addictive behaviours to create a temporary sense of relief or distraction from emotional pain. Substances serve as a form of self-medication, numbing emotions that feel too intense to deal with, such as shame, guilt, or loneliness.

2. Avoidance of Unresolved Feelings

- **Escaping the Past**: Addiction is often a way to avoid confronting painful memories or feelings from childhood. The wounded inner child may have experienced environments where emotional expression was unsafe or punished. As adults, individuals may use substances to avoid feeling vulnerable or re-experiencing the emotional wounds from their past.
- **Dissociation from Trauma**: Addictive behaviours can help a person dissociate from trauma, creating an emotional "numbness" that blocks painful memories from resurfacing. Whether it's through alcohol, drugs, gambling, or other forms of addiction, the individual avoids being fully present with their emotions.

3. Seeking Comfort and Safety

- **Lack of Emotional Safety**: In childhood, if a person lacked emotional safety or was exposed to chaos, they may use addiction in adulthood as a way to feel a false sense of comfort or control. Substances can offer a temporary escape from anxiety and insecurity, recreating a sense of safety that was missing in early life.
- **Self-Soothing**: The wounded inner child, unable to find comfort or security from caregivers, may turn to addictive substances or behaviours to soothe themselves. The

addiction becomes a "safe space" where they can retreat from the pain of the outside world.

4. Seeking Validation through Addiction

- **Low Self-Worth**: The wounded inner child often internalizes feelings of unworthiness or inadequacy, which can lead to seeking external validation through addictive behaviours. This might be through substance use to fit in socially or using substances to boost self-esteem temporarily. The addiction provides a sense of belonging, even if it is artificial.
- **External Fulfilment**: Addictive behaviours may emerge to fill an internal void left by unmet emotional needs in childhood. The wounded inner child, starved for love and validation, seeks fulfilment through substances, hoping to find the love and acceptance they didn't receive growing up.

5. Unresolved Emotional Regulation

- **Difficulty Handling Emotions**: The wounded inner child struggles with emotional regulation due to a lack of proper modelling or support in childhood. Addictive substances offer a way to manage overwhelming feelings of anger, sadness, or anxiety that the inner child doesn't know how to process. Addiction becomes a coping tool when they can't handle intense emotions.

- **Impulsive Behaviour**: The inner child often acts impulsively, seeking immediate gratification through addictive behaviours. The drive to feel better "right now" leads to substance use, compulsive shopping, gambling, or other addictions, as the inner child hasn't learned to delay gratification or sit with discomfort.

6. Self-Destructive Behaviours

- **Punishing Oneself**: A wounded inner child may feel shame and self-blame, believing they are unworthy of happiness or success. This can lead to self-destructive behaviours, including addiction, as a form of self-punishment. Substance abuse becomes a way to reinforce negative beliefs about oneself.
- **Cycle of Shame**: Addiction often perpetuates a cycle of shame, reinforcing the wounded inner child's belief that they are flawed or damaged. The individual may feel deep shame for their addictive behaviour, which in turn drives them back to the addiction to numb the pain of that shame.

7. Fear of Vulnerability

- **Avoiding Emotional Intimacy**: Addiction can serve as a barrier to forming close, intimate relationships. The wounded inner child may fear vulnerability, as it reminds them of past emotional wounds where they were hurt or betrayed. Addictive behaviours

become a way to avoid closeness, preventing the pain of emotional connection while creating a false sense of security.
- **Detachment from Emotions**: The inner child's fear of emotional exposure leads to addiction as a means of avoiding authentic emotional experiences. By staying in the haze of addiction, they avoid being vulnerable, protecting themselves from the potential pain of rejection or failure.

8. Hypervigilance and Control

- **Need for Control**: Growing up in chaotic or abusive environments can leave a person with a wounded inner child feeling powerless. Addiction, while destructive, can offer a false sense of control—controlling how they think, their environment, or their reactions. The person may use substances to manage their emotions or the unpredictability of life.
- **Addiction as a Coping Strategy**: The hypervigilant inner child, always on alert for danger or emotional threats, turns to addiction to manage the stress of constantly feeling unsafe. The substance provides a break from the constant pressure to be in control.

9. Recreating Dysfunctional Patterns

- **Repeating Dysfunctional Cycles**: Often, addiction recreates the same dysfunctional patterns that the wounded inner child experienced in their early life. If their childhood was marked by neglect, abuse, or emotional instability, addiction can serve to repeat these cycles of chaos, reinforcing the unresolved pain and trauma from the past.

- **Attraction to Dysfunction**: The wounded inner child may be unconsciously drawn to chaos, drama, or instability in relationships and environments, which can perpetuate addictive behaviours. Growing up in a volatile environment can make stability feel unfamiliar or even uncomfortable, leading to self-sabotage through addiction.

10. Seeking Escape from Reality

- **Fleeing the Present Moment**: For many people with a wounded inner child, addiction is a way to escape from the present reality, which may feel too painful or unmanageable. The inner child, overwhelmed by unresolved trauma, turns to substances or addictive behaviours to dissociate from the present moment, reliving old emotional wounds or avoiding present challenges.
- **Avoidance of Healing**: Engaging in addiction allows the wounded inner child to avoid the complex process of healing and self-reflection. Instead of confronting the deep-seated pain and beginning the work of healing, they continue using substances as a way to avoid facing those inner wounds.

These examples show how addiction is often more than just a chemical dependency; it can be a coping mechanism for the unresolved emotional wounds of a wounded inner child.

Breaking the Cycle: Healing from Trauma and Addiction

Overcoming the dual challenge of trauma and alcoholism requires a multifaceted approach. Acknowledging the link between trauma and substance use is the first critical step. Healing can be a long, complex process that involves therapy, support, and a commitment to recovery. Some of the most effective interventions include:

- **Trauma-informed therapy**: Therapeutic modalities like Eye Movement Desensitization and Reprocessing (EMDR), Cognitive Behavioural Therapy (CBT), and Somatic Experiencing address both trauma and addiction simultaneously. They help individuals reprocess traumatic memories while developing healthy coping mechanisms.
- **Group Therapy and Peer Support**: Support groups like 12 step fellowships provide a sense of community and understanding among individuals facing similar struggles. Trauma-informed support groups create a safe space to address both trauma and substance abuse. In my experience, this has been a lifeline and an integral part of my recovery. I will devote a chapter to the working of a 12-step programme and some of the myths and false preconceptions around it.

- **Mindfulness and Stress-Reduction Practices**: Techniques like mindfulness meditation, yoga, and deep breathing help regulate the body's stress response, reducing the emotional intensity of trauma-related memories. By becoming more mindful, individuals can learn to sit with discomfort rather than turning to alcohol.
- **Medication-Assisted Treatment (MAT)**: For some, medications like Naltrexone, Acamprosate, or Antabuse can help reduce alcohol cravings, allowing individuals to focus more effectively on their trauma recovery. In my experience, I believe there is a place for medications; however, they only tackle the physical symptoms of alcoholism, and, as we will see in a later chapter, the main problem of alcohol centres in mind.

Conclusion: The Road to Recovery

The intersection of trauma and alcoholism is a complex, painful journey that many endure, often in silence. But recovery is possible. The key lies in understanding the deep-rooted connections between trauma and addiction and treating both issues with compassion and care. By addressing the underlying trauma, individuals can find a path to healing that does not require alcohol as a crutch. Healing from trauma is not about erasing the past but learning to live with it in a way that no longer controls the present.

The key to breaking free from addiction is not just addressing the substance use itself but also healing the emotional pain that drives it. Recovery often involves inner child work, therapy, and learning healthier ways to cope with emotions and trauma.

There is hope, and we recover; I want to give you a massive injection of proper light and hope here. I never imagined I would be writing my memoirs to help others get free from the clutches of addiction, and I never thought I would say alcohol made me the badass recovery warrior I am today.

I have worked through my demons, and I am a free woman, and you can be too.

The following chapters focus on my final rehab and new beginnings, and believe me if I can do it, so can you or your loved one.

There is hope and freedom, and I believe in you.

Rehab attempt 2

As if one rehab with its joy and experience wasn't enough, I had to return for round 2.

This is a common practice amongst people with an addiction if it's affordable. Most rehabs cost thousands of pounds, and in my case, it was £7500 for a 2-week stay in Costa del rehab.

My parents were kind enough to lend me the funds, and I would pay them back with the proceeds from my house sale.

Did I need rehab?

Yes, as I couldn't separate myself from alcohol now, not even for 24 hours, and I would suffer withdrawal.

The sudden withdrawal from alcohol can be fatal for those who are drink-dependent, and this was a box I now ticked with flying colours.

I felt like a complete loser as I stood there waiting for my lift to the cure, and this is documented in Chapter 1, so let's get straight into my arrival at Rehab 2.

This rehab was more aesthetically pleasing. I was immediately greeted by a well-dressed woman who took me to the admitting room and asked me what to expect during my sabbatical.

In all honesty, at that point, I would have spent two weeks in hell if it stopped me from feeling this emotional torture.

After admission, I was escorted upstairs and shown around. I looked out of my bedroom window while the staff went through my belongings to check I hadn't sneaked in a bottle of 40% proof, and what pissed me off more was why didn't I think of that? Damn, I could have hidden a bottle in my case lining.

The rest of the day was spent either in the smoking room or the recreational room.

It was in the recreational room that I first met P, another alcoholic from the Northeast of the UK. Although I was in a relationship with a new man (long term, two weeks), I couldn't let an opportunity pass for true love, so this was the beginning of a true love story in Rehab.

Note: It is frowned upon in Rehab and also a terrible idea for two people with an addiction to come together who are both equally fucked up and looking for happiness in withdrawal; I mean, what could go wrong.

The first week was spent mainly feeling the effects of withdrawal and what is lovingly called "doing your rattle."

My days were spent sweating and shaking while watching crap movies with other poor souls.

I met some beautiful souls there and listened to their stories about their upbringing in this establishment.

Note: Not one person I met in there and throughout my drinking days and sobriety ever said when I grow up, I want to be an addict/alcoholic. Not one person ever said I know I have arrived in life when I have been a visitor to rehab. One thing that every person does have in common is they all used/drank to self-medicate, especially in the latter years.

The drink/drug helped at first and made them feel more confident, alive, and able to cope. However, this is the cycle of doom as the more they drank, the more they received negative consequences and needed more drink to cope.

I have met hundreds of substance-dependent people, and I have not met one who doesn't have a story of trauma and pain.

In my experience, society tries to treat the consequences of drinking, such as medication and abstinence. What it doesn't often look at is the pain and why the person drinks. What does the drink/drug give them that life doesn't?

I have seen many people just stop drinking and not work on their trauma and issues, and some of these unfortunate souls are no longer with us as they didn't treat the cause, the trauma, and life became too painful, so they opted to leave the planet.

Week 1 passed painfully slowly, and although medicated again with Librium, withdrawal from alcohol is painful, physically and emotionally.

This is another point to make: addiction is a cunning foe. Why?

I went through withdrawal again and again and again in my decades of drinking, and the pain never got more accessible, so why do it again? This is another example of the insanity of taking the first drink.

Week 1 was complete, and P was already promoted to the first floor, where the therapy begins, so I already had a future husband downstairs. I know how insane that sounds, but in those final 12 months of drinking, my mind was in 1000 bits floating in the galaxy somewhere, and I had lost my sanity with it.

I had a new bedroom downstairs, which wasn't as lovely as my previous room but acceptable.

There were around 10 of us, mainly alcoholics but a few addicts also, and addiction is an addition, so we are all in the same boat, or sinking Titanic.

The food was terrific, and we had a sweet corner where we all contributed from our escorted visits to the local shop.

There is a lot of camaraderie and laughter in a rehab facility, and even though there are also many tears and sadness, we were all united by our common problem: self-medicating our lives to the point of losing our lives.

Rehab activities

Believe it or not, there is a weekly planner in Rehab, and we also had chores to complete. I guess it's not slave labour. It's more about keeping a routine, although I did find it amusing that this was the most expensive place I had ever stayed at, and it didn't come with hotel services.

Shop visits

We were allowed to go to the shop after each day of therapy sessions. It was a short walk, and we were escorted on and off the premises, yet we were still breathalysed after every shop visit. Did anyone achieve success in these visits?

Yep, one man managed to buy a bottle of Vodka, threw it into a bush in the gardens, and retrieved it later that night. This resulted in a ban on all daily shop visits.

The shop outings were a welcome distraction and something to look forward to. In Rehab, you tend to get your appetite back, and the sugar cravings when detoxing are evil, so everyone comes back with buckets of sweets.

Therapy sessions

These sessions were mainly group sessions, with one exception being my last day.

The group sessions were about sharing our stories and homework around step work. I will go into detail about step work in the next chapter. I managed to complete steps 1-3 in rehab, although when I got a sponsor, she told me I had to start again.

I remember one session becoming very upset as we had to share a traumatic event, and I had many to choose from. I mentioned sexual abuse, and one guy kept probing for the full story like I was on an episode of a talk show, and he needed the juicy details. I told him to Fuk off and walked around the garden for an hour to cool off, accompanied by P, who was also fuming, bless him.

My final session was with an alcohol counsellor who spent the hour talking about how a relationship with P was not a good idea on the outside. I thought she was jealous, which is hilarious now as I was far from sane at the time and talked about a disaster pending.

AA meetings

I was allowed to attend AA meetings in this Rehab as they were held on the grounds. I will delve more into this in the next chapter.

Romance

Yep, this is an official activity that goes off in Rehabs worldwide. I had my future husband (or so I thought) wait for it, and he asked me to marry him outside a betting shop on one of our shop visits. It's not exactly the love story of dreams, but I said yes, and so all we had to do was stay sober, and we would have our dream life. Some of the others in the unit bought cards with congratulations. I think it's safe to say that none of us were thinking here.

People who never made it

Unfortunately, it's heartbreaking to report that many people who joined me at the Rehab are no longer with us. Sometimes, you hear through friends, but most commonly through Facebook, where either they committed suicide or drank themselves to death. Either way was a way out and sometimes the only way people knew how to get sober.

Every alcoholic takes their last drink someday, and some of us get to talk about theirs, hence the book.

The final Rehab activity

The food there was excellent, like old-school dinners, with plenty of cake and custard.

Most people put on a significant amount of weight in Rehab due to getting their taste back, refuelling for their next alcohol run, and boredom.

I say Refuelling as there are people who attend rehab as a regular visitor, often paid for by family as respite. They participate as an inpatient for months and then go out again for another year or more of active addiction.

Family visits

My family was allowed to visit during week 2, and my mum came with the girls to take me out to town. I will never forget the look on her face when I went to the door, heartbreak and sadness. Alcoholism affects the entire family, and we have talked about this in recent years. My mum said I looked awful and so lost.

I am ashamed to report that for the majority of our outing, I talked about what an excellent person P was and how we were going to support each other in sobriety when we got out of rehab. I was amazed that my mum and kids didn't share my enthusiasm, and why would they? This plan was insane, and so was I.

After the visit, I was breathalysed and returned to the recreational room to tell my newfound friends and P all about it.

Leaving Rehab

My two weeks were completed, and I was leaving sober. I was petrified that being there was like a safety bubble from the outside world. There were no temptations, and I had been surrounded by support for two weeks: zero stress, lots of food, and P on demand.

I was going to miss P, so that evening, I returned for an AA meeting not to stay sober but to see P.

I mentioned in a previous chapter that my future sponsor had told me I had lost the power to choose to drink, so you would have thought that I would get a grip and focus on my sobriety as if my life depended on it. It did, and yet again, here I was, putting a man ahead of everything as a distraction and relapse prevention aid.

Church

I went home, and my mum stayed with us for several more days. My mum had lived at my house during my stay, and I am so grateful as I was scared to death I would drink again. I came out on Friday, and that night, I had the most vivid dream of attending a particular church on Sunday morning at 10:30. The dream felt like an instruction, and I can't explain how and why; please take my word for it; it was a loving order and one that I obeyed.

The church was not the service I expected; it was lively, vibrant, and full of laughter and love. I remember the live band, and everyone stood clapping and singing, and in that moment, I knew I was saved, and I knew I wouldn't drink again. It wasn't that I knew I couldn't. It was because I knew that I didn't need to. I knew I was loved deeply in that church, and it made me sob continuously for the entire service. The big man had saved my sorry ass yet again and set me free. That day it changed me in so many ways. That was the day I began to wake up to reality and accept the task in front of me, getting sober for good and for all and getting my sanity and my life back. I knew I had divine strength to do that now, but I also knew this was only the first step on my journey. I was willing and ready.

I hope this does not put the reader off. This is my story, and I am telling it from my heart and in complete truth.

P ending

My relationship with P ended as I realized I had to put my recovery first, and P had already relapsed a few times. We have kept in touch sporadically over the years. I will get an occasional Facebook message from his new account. P always said he was in another Rehab, and this time he had got it, followed by another year or more of silence. I haven't heard from P for over two years now, and I pray he is still with us and has finally submitted and accepted help.

P, like many others suffering addiction, had horrendous abuse at a young age and cannot let that go. Sadly, when this happens, the person holds on to that pain so tightly they can't let go, and the resentment inside destroys them.

The Recovery (getting out of the pit of addiction)

For this alcoholic, there was only one way: the steps.

Note I refer to my sponsor, S, in this chapter, and I would like to say I am eternally grateful for her patience with me in my early days. I was an absolute pain in the ass, and she had to be strict with me as I needed it to save my life, thank you.

Step 1.

We admitted we were powerless over alcohol and that our lives had become unmanageable.

This was the beginning of my emotional sobriety. I had read the text of how a 12-step fellowship works in Rehab number 1 and thought it was written for anyone apart from me. It was old and outdated and felt utterly irrelevant to me. I was wrong in every way; it may as well have been named Mandy's Book of Life and Destruction.

I had been to enough meetings in AA to know what the steps said as they are hung on scrolls at every meeting. I thought easy, and I get them all, so I don't have to work them as I know it all, as usual.

I knew nothing at all, and at this point in my life, I was finally willing to listen. This willingness came from years of pain and many failed attempts at going alone and failing miserably.

I was fresh out of Rehab number 2, and quite honestly, if someone had said go over there and stand on your head for an hour in the pissing rain to get sober for good, I would have wholeheartedly agreed.

This is commonly known as the gift of desperation, and I knew that I had two choices

1. Work this program of recovery with everything I had or
2. Die
    This may sound dramatic, but it was true, and I chose option 1, though many do not.
    I listened and followed the guidance of my sponsor, who took no prisoners and accepted no bollox or manipulation tactics as they didn't work with her.
    My sponsor, S, had seen it all before and had sobriety, and she had agreed to take me through the 12 steps.
    It was mind-blowing how she related each chapter to me and asked if I identified, to which I was a nodding dog, for I related to every word.

First, I had to smash the illusion that I could control my driving independently. It's remarkable that even after all of the evidence of losing control of my drinking, I was still hanging on to the hope that one day I would be able to.

I can laugh about this now, but there was no laughter then. My sponsor smashed this illusion into a million pieces. I could still argue my pathetic case that there was one time I had been out with friends around twelve years ago and had only one glass of wine. S laughed, but I didn't find it amusing at all. We then spent a further hour going through the thousand other times I had drunk way more than one.

I have a medical science degree and am a self-professed nerd who loves facts and figures. I had done extensive research h over the past few decades, and the numbers for the probability of lack of control were not adding up in my favour.

I understood this to the letter as I had lost control of my drinking decades ago, and I was done with saying otherwise; it had beaten me. I was still Billy Big Bollox, and I could identify as some of those stories my sponsor went through with me from the introductory text of a 12-step book demonstrated examples of strong-willed businesspeople. With me being a highflyer, I could relate, and yes, my drinking had escalated somewhat.

As I write, I am smiling as back then, I was so full of ego and pride, still hanging on by a thread of hope that one day I would be able to drink like regular drinkers.

It's alarming I thought this, and yet, from my experience, I am not alone; many new people to recovery are still kicking and screaming their denial.

The evidence clearly states throughout this book I had lost control, and my ducks were not in a row. They were swimming, pissed up in the sea, heading towards Peru.

What is Alcoholism?

The first thing to mention is from experience, alcoholism doesn't ever go away. I have never heard a real alcoholic say they just woke up one day and decided enough was enough, put the plug in the jug, and lived happily ever after.

Alcoholism is a progressive illness, and mental obsession makes it so difficult for individuals to quit drinking. Alcoholism is described as an illness with both a physical craving and a mental obsession. Once an alcoholic takes a drink, they lose the ability to control the quantity, leading to binge drinking and destructive behaviour.

I can relate as my drinking career had taken off to epic levels, and I obsessed with drinking for years. In my lifetime, I can count on one hand the number of times I have had one drink, and yet I still kept bringing this up with S, so it was a long first meeting.

My sponsor was incredibly patient as she continued emphasizing the hopeless nature of untreated alcoholism, explaining that willpower alone is usually insufficient to solve the problem. Alcoholics tend to repeat the cycle of promising to quit, only to relapse, because they are unable to break free of the obsession without help.

This is the crux of the problem: of mental obsession that sounds like me in my head saying this time it will be different; you will only drink on the weekend, this time you will stop after 2, etc., etc.

From experience, kicking the habit for a few days can be done, and although painful, it can be achieved, but the obsession to drink is the killer. That obsession sounded like this.

How can I drink tonight,

How can I hide it

What time can I have a drink

Why can't I have a drink

I need a drink

I want a drink

Drink, drink, drink, you get the picture. I couldn't go a day or even an hour without thinking about booze, and it was consumed every thought of every minute.

The Solution:

It took a long time for me to see and fully accept (not just lip service) but fully accept that I was an alcoholic and that I would NEVER be able to drink like an average person. I was both relieved and mortified.

S let me have a moment to let it sing in and reassured me that the solution to alcoholism involves a combination of spiritual principles and fellowship with other alcoholics. Central to this approach is the belief in a higher power and the willingness to surrender personal control over alcohol. The solution requires a personal spiritual transformation and mutual support from others who share similar struggles.

I had finally truly and honestly admitted I was completely powerless over alcohol. The solution was out there as many others had achieved sobriety, and S reassured me I could too if I remained teachable and shut the fek up long enough to listen.

I had to be willing, and I was now, as I couldn't live like this anymore. S told me I needed to believe in a higher power and live spiritually.

Some people can't accept this, but I found it reassuring, and I feel blessed that I wasn't one of those alcoholics who couldn't believe in a higher power.

I knew I had been living my life under a cloud of darkness, immorality, and lies, so I would welcome a more spiritual life, as would those who were around me.

Many people have negative previous experiences with religion and have preconceived ideas of fire and brimstone. I have always believed in a god and, for many years, have used him as the 4th emergency service.

God, get me out of this mess, please.

For any readers who may have a problem with alcohol, a higher power can be nature, the universe, or a god of your understanding. It just has to be spiritual, as human power won't do. If there were a human on this earth that could have stopped me from drinking, it would have been my children, and it wasn't so that no other human would do.

The Fellowship of AA:

I had been attending meetings without blinkers and judgment. I found them essential, especially in the evenings, as my evenings had always revolved around drink and oblivion, so this would keep me busy.

The fellowship aspect of AA. Alcoholics can achieve sobriety by helping each other. By sharing their experiences, struggles, and successes, alcoholics find strength and hope through their collective experience. The mutual support system of AA is crucial, as it provides members with accountability and guidance.

I remember coming into the fellowship, fearing losing all my friends. I was told that I would lose fair-weather friends, but I would gain a new set of real friends, and I had no idea how accurate that turned out to be.

Key points I had learned.

- Alcoholism is a progressive disease that cannot be cured, but it can be arrested.
- Willpower alone is not enough to overcome alcoholism.
- Spiritual principles, including belief in a higher power and surrender, are essential for recovery.
- Fellowship and mutual support through AA are vital components of maintaining sobriety.

I thought I had done amazingly well, and yet our first meeting wasn't over yet; as with most alcoholics, I needed the point hammered home. S reinforced the idea that many alcoholics struggle with accepting the fact that they cannot control their drinking. Despite their repeated failures to moderate or quit drinking, alcoholics often deceive themselves into thinking they can regain control over alcohol.

I wouldn't say I liked this as I was getting bored and thinking S must think I am stupid (oh, the ego). So, she continued to stress that self-deception, denial, and the illusion of power are the hallmarks of alcoholism, and complete acceptance of powerlessness is essential to recovery.

I was asked to give examples of how I had previously controlled my drinking. I thought that was good. I now have a chance to show S how successful I have been. (Self-denial ran through me like Blackpool rock)

I gave my examples, including when I was a child with my dad's vodka and lime; I'm laughing here as, at the time, I still thought this was a perfect example of control. I was disappointed when S said, "And how's that been working out for your Mandy"? S went on to describe how alcoholics often convince themselves that they will eventually be able to drink like other people, yet this belief is based on self-delusion. The reality is that once alcoholics start drinking, they have no control over how much they consume.

Throughout the book, I have given many examples of how I tried to control/stop drinking and failed. I always would say next week, next month, and next year, and it never happened.

I could never have one drink and always ended up smashed. This part of the book explains why and that every alcoholic lives in self-delusion and denial, and many take it to the grave.

I asked the question as many recruits do.

Why is it essential to prevent myself from being powerless, as it was never on my bucket list again? S laughed (what a bitch, eh)

I learned that self-knowledge wouldn't fix me. She insisted that knowing my problem intellectually is insufficient; acceptance on a deeper, emotional level is critical. I disagreed slightly here as I had learned a fair amount in Rehab one and set myself up for a fall as S said, "Well, that didn't exactly work out either, did it?" As much as I disliked her at this point for being rude, I had to agree.

I often say that I needed every drink I ever took to get to this point—the point of admitting that I am utterly powerless against alcohol. My best attempts at staying away from the first drink failed every time, and I always ended up back to burning my life down.

It was during this meeting that we went through what a regular drinker, heavy drinker, and alcoholic are and which category I fall into.

As you can imagine, I clung to the fact that I may be a heavy drinker. Most alcoholics will cling to this fact as let's face it, nobody wants to be an alcoholic. At this point, S rolled her eyes, and this wasn't the first time. I learned that heavy drinkers could stop, for example, if they had a health scare, and S reminded me that a brain aneurysm is a health scare, so that put me firmly in the alcoholic category.

For the real alcoholic, there are no triggers, and as soon as I began my disagreement speech, S hammered this point home and said there are no triggers for the real alcoholic.

I had hidden behind triggers for years, and she smashed my delusions into pieces.

I drank in a relationship and out

I drank when I had money and no money

I drank when I was happy and sad

I drank when my life was tremendous and shit (you get the picture)

The Mental Obsession

This mental obsession with booze takes many alcoholics to their graves, and S stressed again that alcoholism is not just a physical craving but also a mental obsession. Even after periods of abstinence, alcoholics may be overwhelmed by thoughts of drinking. The mind plays tricks, convincing the individual that they can handle just one drink. This mental obsession is seen as a critical feature of alcoholism, and its why alcoholics so often relapse after periods of sobriety; due to this painful truth, I was sobbing….again. If it were as simple as a physical craving, we would all have three days of pain, and that would be it: have a happy life. The big book would be 1 page long and easy.

It is the mental obsession that convinced me over and over again to drink again. I fully understood now why, after my first rehab and three weeks of abstinence, I drank again. I had convinced myself it was a good idea, which was insane.

The Need for a Spiritual Solution

S explained that a "psychic change" or spiritual experience is necessary for recovery. Alcoholics must undergo a complete shift in their thinking and behaviour. This can only happen when they admit that they are powerless over alcohol and that their lives have become unmanageable.

Without this spiritual awakening, many alcoholics will continue to relapse, as the root of their problem is not just their drinking but their inability to control the mental obsession that precedes it. The book hints at the Twelve Steps of AA, which offer a path toward this spiritual transformation.

I could buy into this 100% as I was desperate to feel better and lose the mental obsession. I had managed to fuk most of my life up, so if someone could give me a new rule book, I was all in.

Key lessons so far:

Self-delusion: Many alcoholics deceive themselves into thinking they can drink moderately or regain control over alcohol.

- **Full acceptance**: True recovery begins only when an alcoholic fully concedes that they are powerless over alcohol.
- **Mental obsession**: Alcoholism is not just a physical dependence but a mental obsession that compels people to drink even when they know it's destructive.
- **Spiritual solution**: The only lasting solution for alcoholics is a spiritual awakening, a complete transformation of their thinking, and reliance on a higher power.
-

S had made me concede fully that I had zero power against alcohol, and my life was not only unmanageable, it was utter chaos, and I was not only insane but also an utterly selfish nob. (who knew) I now know that I had fully conceded to being powerless, and there was no way I could control my drinking through willpower alone. The mental obsession is the actual problem, and the solution lies in a spiritual awakening that frees the alcoholic from this obsession, allowing them to live a life of sobriety.

The Problem of Spirituality for the Alcoholic

Many alcoholics struggle with the idea of turning their will and life over to a higher power. Some atheists or agnostics are unsure or unwilling to believe in a spiritual solution.

Many alcoholics initially come to AA with deep doubts or even outright rejection of religious or spiritual ideas. However, S asserted that open-mindedness is crucial to recovery, so they asked me if I had any thoughts on a higher power or any prejudices or preconceived notions about spirituality.

Suppose you are reading this and are put off by the idea of a higher power. In my sponsor's words, "There is a god, and it is not you."

The gift of desperation is truly a gift, and for me, it took soul destruction and utter misery. I was ready and willing to believe that a higher power could help me run my life; I wasn't exactly doing a grand job myself.

The Limits of Self-Will

S stressed that self-will alone is insufficient to recover from alcoholism. She described how alcoholics often rely on their intellect or willpower to control their drinking, only to fail repeatedly. This failure stems from the inability to address the deeper mental obsession with alcohol. The authors suggest that alcoholics must accept help from a power greater than themselves to overcome this mental obsession.

From experience, alcoholics have cast iron wills. It takes a will of iron to continue drinking when puke is in your mouth, but they know they will feel better if they can get that drink down.

Many alcoholics are baffled as to why they can't stop, as many are highly successful people who have managed to win in all aspects of life other than booze.

A Universal Concept of God

I believe everyone somehow knows and understands that there is something out there, some higher power in the universe.

I don't have a traditional view of God. I was happy and comfortable with this concept as I could create my conception of a higher power. The goal was to surrender personal control and seek guidance and strength from something greater than me. I slowly realized that I'm not the centre of the universe.

From experience, many alcoholics start by being willing to believe and take small steps toward spiritual growth. This willingness opens the door to recovery and spiritual transformation.

I often say to new people wanting to get sober and look at the trees, stars, and nature. I ask them if they are more powerful than nature and the night sky. The answer is always no, so I say know there is a greater intelligence out there and believe that is enough. In my experience, my god doesn't make hard and fast rules and will help regardless of name.

The exact nature of one's belief is less important than the willingness to let go of self-will and embrace a spiritual solution.

The "Spiritual Experience"

I asked what a spiritual experience is and why I need one.

I must be hilarious as S laughed again. She could see from outside, looking at the absolute bollox I had made of my life so far, and still ask why I needed a spiritual experience.

The answer

To remove the mental obsession to drink and live not exist.

I had my first spiritual experience before my aneurysm surgery and disregarded it.

My god gave me another chance during the church service the week I came out of rehab; he had never let me down, even when I used him as an emergency service hundreds of times.

I was due for another spiritual awakening, so bring it on.

S asked me again if I would go to any lengths and remain open-minded. I answered yes, and she reassured me that I don't need to have all the answers regarding spirituality from the beginning as its progress, not perfection. I do believe she may have read my mind, as with most alcoholics, I can overthink everything.

Recovery is seen as a lifelong journey, and each step toward spiritual growth helps to strengthen sobriety. Alcoholics are encouraged to take action, whether it's starting with prayer, meditation, or simply being open to the idea of a higher power.

I needed a psychic change as I was a glass half complete and a total of resentments.

I had a bad case of the old poor me poor me pour me a drink.

Note. I would not say I am religious; I aim for spirituality. I think religion is often used as a means of control and rule. My god isn't like that, and I believe in gods in all of us, and we can all have our relationship with the creator; even if you prefer to see the source as the night sky or ocean, it doesn't matter.

Key Points

1. **Open-Mindedness and Willingness**: Alcoholics are encouraged to let go of rigid thinking and be open to the idea of a higher power, even if they don't have a clear understanding of what that means at first.
2. **Higher Power of Personal Understanding**: people can define their concept of a higher power. It doesn't have to align with any specific religious doctrine—it can be as simple as the strength of the group or nature itself.
3. **The Spiritual Experience**: Recovery from alcoholism often requires a profound change in thinking and behaviour, which is typically achieved through some form of spiritual awakening. This can happen dramatically or gradually.
4. **Mental Obsession Overcome by Spiritual Solutions**: Alcoholics cannot overcome their mental obsession with alcohol through self-will alone. They hope to be free from the obsession to drink only by surrendering to a higher power.
5. **The Role of Action**: Spiritual growth is not just about belief but also about taking concrete actions—such as working the steps, helping others, and remaining open to

spiritual principles—that help bring the necessary psychic change for recovery.

S went through a recap; she likes repetition, and I find listening hard. I was willing, and I did believe in a higher power and found it to be a relief that something else could take the reins of my life. I had to stop analysing everything and trust in the process, and I had no choice, so that's what I decided to do as, let's face it, nothing else had worked, and it was this or death.

It amazes me that the writer of the BigBook spent the first 57 pages of the introductory text of 164 pages on step one. This made me realize that alcoholics are in denial and need it hammering home again and again for 57 pages to submit, get off their pity pot, and get to work. I was no different, and by the end of page 57, I needed a break.

My sponsor allowed 10 minutes, and we cracked on with step 2.

Step 2

We believed that a power greater than ourselves could restore us to sanity.

At this point in my life, I had proved my insanity around alcohol with flying colours, bells, and whistles.

I knew there was a higher intelligence, which I chose to call God, and if this program had worked for millions of people worldwide, it could have worked for Mandy.

I had to believe that my sanity could be restored and completely free. My sponsor told me to look around the rooms of AA, where I would see plenty of evidence.

Step 3

We decided to turn our will and lives over to the care of God as we understood him.

I was exhausted at this point, as in one sitting, we had gone through steps 1 and 2, but S encouraged me to continue for another hour. I now see why, although I thought she was a fekin taskmaster then.

I had three questions to answer

1. That I was an alcoholic and couldn't manage my own life. Tick
2. That probably no human power could have relieved my alcoholism tick
3. That god could and would if he were sought tick
This step was both a relief and painful. The pain came from understanding how selfishness and self-centredness were the root of my problem.
Alcoholism is often called in AA as the disease of self, and this was true for me. I was consumed in self, self-pity, self-destruction, self-delusion, and self-seeking, ouch.
I had used my toolkit of manipulation to try and run this show called Life, and if anyone dared to disagree or step in my way, they would be sorry.

I had to eliminate this self-problem and colossal ego, and what a task this was.
I couldn't; we had to hand this task to a higher power. If I could have, I would have saved myself years of

pain and stopped being an ass, but I hadn't/couldn't.

On that day, I handed my life over to God to take the reins, and that's the relief as thank fee I wasn't steering the Titanic anymore.

That day was complete, and I had officially worked steps 1-3.

I had homework, which seemed easy enough. I was to write down a list of all the people who had pissed me off in the past, why I'm angry at them, what they did, and how this affects me.

This was pleasing to hear as I loved getting on my pity bot and complaining about how unfair life has been for me, poor me.

Step 4

Make a searching and fearless moral inventory of ourselves

Step 5

Admitted to God and another human being the exact nature of our wrongs.

S had left me two weeks after the last meeting, and I was under strict instructions to attend as many AA meetings as possible.

I attended a meeting most evenings in those early weeks as I was lost. My usual routine was no more, and this in itself played havoc with my OCD and past decades of drinking. Meetings were a lifesaver and provided the necessary structure for my new life.

I arrived bright and early at S's house and ready to let her know the reasons why my life had been so shit, and she would then understand and probably apologize for being so harsh with me in our previous meeting.

I was very mistaken, as little did I know we were doing steps 4 and 5 that day, and it would be brutal. I was about to discover how I show up in the world, not my usual BS.

Making a Moral Inventory

My task was to complete a "searching and fearless moral inventory." This step involves looking hard at one's fundamental flaws, resentments, fears, and harmful actions. It asks alcoholics to reflect deeply on their past behaviours and attitudes, acknowledging the root causes of their drinking and other destructive habits.

I was under strict guidance that I must let go of their self-centeredness and examine my relationships with others to identify patterns of harm. This inventory is a way to uncover the internal causes of alcoholism and to understand how personal defects of character have contributed to the problem.

Resentments:

Resentment is one of the most dangerous emotions for alcoholics, as it fuels negative thoughts and feelings, leading to harmful behaviours like drinking. I had homework to systematically identify resentments by listing people, institutions, or situations that have caused anger or bitterness, and we Alcoholics are we could analyse how these resentments have affected my life, relationships, and self-esteem.

I had tons of resentments, and I let S know precisely what they were, who caused them, and how it made me feel.

It turned out very different from what I expected as we looked at my part in each resentment. Holy Monkeys.

It took hours until I could finally see my part in each resentment, and S helped me (kicking and whinging) to see clearly that I had a part, usually a massive one. S insisted on brutal honesty and willingness, and after a few hours and lots of tea, we got there, but we weren't finished, groan.

Fears:

The inventory should also include a review of personal fears. These fears often drive many of the alcoholic's harmful actions and thoughts. Alcoholics are encouraged to acknowledge these fears and recognize how they have controlled their behaviour.

So, S skilfully made me see that I was driven by fear and that my self-centredness and manipulation toolkit were in full force due to fear of everything.

The main one is fear of losing control. The irony is that I was not in control of anything,

Fear of abandonment. It made sense as before anyone could abandon me, I abandoned them.

Sexual Conduct and Harm to Others:

In addition to resentments and fears, the inventory should cover personal relationships, particularly romantic and sexual ones. Alcoholics must examine how their actions have hurt others, whether through dishonesty, selfishness, or manipulation.

This one took another few hours as I had been a complete slag for many years, and my conduct had been shameful.

The main point of a step 4 inventory is to highlight character defects.

I had a lot of selfishness, manipulation, lies, deceit, fear, massive ego, and general round shithead.

This may sound awful to many, but it's necessary as I had lived my life destroying others' peace as well as my own, and until I could see the error of my ways, nothing would change, and I needed change to live.

Many people put off doing step 4 as it's painful, but it's vital and completely freeing once done.

I experienced relief after we had talked through every resentment and my part in it, and we now had a list of character defects as long as my arm.

Confession

Step 5 involves admitting "to God, to ourselves, and to another human being the exact nature of our wrongs." This step is crucial because it helps alcoholics stop hiding from their past and release the guilt and shame associated with their behaviours.

Many people put this step off for months and even years, but I wanted to do it. I have always been a person who would rather rip the plaster off quickly, and I was desperate to get emotional sobriety.

From experience, willingness is a gift, and I had that gift at this time in abundance.

The process is vital for the following reasons

- It breaks the isolation that many alcoholics feel, allowing them to connect with others and receive guidance.
- It helps reduce the ego and pride that often prevent personal growth.
- It brings a sense of relief and freedom by letting go of secrets causing emotional pain.

Relief and Spiritual Growth:

Completing Step 5 often leads to a sense of relief and clarity, which was so true for me. I could finally get things out and see how I show up in life. I could now move forward in life and begin to feel unburdened by my past mistakes, enabling me to move forward with a new sense of purpose. I could start to release the negative emotions that have been fuelling my addiction.

I had been entirely open and honest both to my sponsor and, for the first time, to myself. I was done with the self-deception, and I was ready to swallow some uncomfortable truths. as hard as it was, I was prepared to release the guilt and shame of my past. I had to continue my journey to freedom and open the door to emotional healing and spiritual progress.

These steps, although touchy, are essential in breaking the cycle of denial and self-deception that often accompanies alcoholism.

After this session with my sponsor, I was given steps 6 and 7 instructions.

I felt like the world's weight had been lifted from my shoulders, and I was becoming a better person and beginning to smile. Most of all, when I looked in the mirror, I saw a soul, my soul.

Steps 6 and 7: Addressing Character Defects (Pages 71-76)

Step 6: We are entirely ready to have God remove our shortcomings.

1. Humbly asked him to remove our shortcomings.

Step 6: Becoming Ready for Change

That evening, after returning from my sponsor's house, I had a moment with God and let him have every character defect of mine.

Was I ready and willing?

Yes, yes, and yes, I had lived in torment for so long, and my way of living hadn't worked and had led me to drink my way through a pitiful existence.

Step 6 requires individuals to become "entirely ready" to have their higher power remove their character defects. This step follows the self-examination and admission of wrongs from Steps 4 and 5. The *Big Book* emphasizes that alcoholics must fully accept their shortcomings, be willing to let go of them, and trust that a higher power can help them change.

The text acknowledges that some defects may be challenging to surrender because they have been coping mechanisms for many years. However, the willingness to change is vital to spiritual progress.

Step 7: Humility and Asking for Help

Step 7 involves humbly asking a higher power to remove these shortcomings. The focus here is on humility—alcoholics must recognize that they cannot remove these defects on their own and must rely on spiritual help.

I recognized and admitted that I had been an absolute prize nob to many people who had the honour of entering my life or misfortune. I had many character flaws and had been highly selfish in my ways. Many of my wrongdoings stemmed from fears, and the largest one was fear of rejection and losing control. From these fears, I had been resentful, miserable, and generally like an angry wasp, and I was ready to give these fears to God.

There is a common misconception that faith and fear are opposites. I believe that God wants me to face my fears with the faith that he has got me, which has turned out to be true in all aspects of my life.

In my experience, after I asked my higher power to remove my shortcomings and finally asked for help, not as an emergency service but as my father, the help came.

I use this in everyday life as when I complain about someone else and how they should live their life, I know there is something in me. These days, I often pray God changes me.

I have given up mopping up the sea as it doesn't work and is exhausting.

This doesn't mean I am a pushover. It means I respect and value my peace now, and I don't have to win an argument or a debate. We all have our opinions, and I am not usually the one that handles fixing everyone else. Just work on being a better human being day by day.

It's progress, not perfection.

Anthony DeMello puts it best.

Stop trying to recarpet the world and change your slippers.

Steps 8 and 9: Making Amends

Step 8: Make a list of all persons we harmed and become willing to make amends to them all.

Step 9. Made direct amends to such people wherever possible, except when doing so would injure them or others.

Step 8: Willingness to Make Amends

Step 8 involves making a list of all the people the alcoholic has harmed and becoming willing to make amends to them. This step continues the process of taking responsibility for past actions, which began with the moral inventory in Step 4. Alcoholics are encouraged to approach this step with honesty and a genuine willingness to repair the damage done.

I had guidance from S regarding making amends and that although this may be difficult, it is essential to healing broken relationships and regaining self-respect. The willingness to make amends, even before action, is crucial to spiritual growth.

This part of the program was the part I had been dreading.

In my drinking, I had hurt so many people; I had let them down and sometimes even destroyed their faith in humankind.

It was a nightmare coming into people's lives. I remember the Taylor Swift song "Blank Space " and the line in the song "Darling I'm a nightmare dressed like a daydream. "Oh yes, I could relate to that.

I had listened to my sponsor's guidelines on who to include in my list of amends and knew that although I needed to do this for my sobriety, I wasn't relishing the prospect.

The guideline stated that I must only amend if it would do more good than harm. I heard Mandy, you don't have to make amends. Then, as a good saleswoman, I can convince myself and others this was acceptable. It wasn't to my sponsor, although there were a few to which that rule applied.

Luckily, my sponsor had kept a list of potential amends from my steps 4 and 5 (how nice)

I had to make genuine and heartfelt amends to every person I had hurt (ouch)

I was informed I had to return to the drawing board with the list of 5 and get it accurate. It may sound like my sponsor, S, is awful, but I needed a kick, and she regularly gave me that kick. I took my tiny list away and added approximately 100 names to it and then reviewed it again with S, and my instructions were to get cracking.

Step 9: Making Direct Amends

Step 9 calls for alcoholics to make direct amends to those they have harmed, wherever possible, except when doing so would cause harm to others. This step involves more than simply saying sorry; it requires sincere efforts to repair the damage caused by past behaviour. In some cases, financial restitution may be necessary, while emotional or relationship healing may be needed in others.

I needed to approach my amends with humility and without expectation of forgiveness. The focus is on taking responsibility for my actions and seeking to right past wrongs, not gaining approval or validation.

However, there are cases where direct amends might cause harm—for example, revealing past actions that could hurt another person. Advises caution from S.

The process of my amends was lengthy, and I set about making them straight away, but to this day, I haven't been able to make all of my amends; why?

Some of these amendments will show up at the right time, and a text or visit request may not be appropriate.

I will include some of my amends to my loved ones.

My Girls

I have always been there physically for my daughters, but not emotionally. I always provided, and they never went without. It was tough as a single mum, but I was always in a rush. I worked full-time and had to get everything else done so I could start drinking.

If I could turn back time and change this, I would in a heartbeat, but I can't, so I made my amends with the hope that they could forgive me.

My youngest daughter will not speak to me and has cut me out of her life. In my early sobriety, I found it hard to regulate emotions and tried to start putting some rules in place. This came after years of anything for an easy life. I didn't get it right, unfortunately, and we are estranged. I have felt intense guilt and shame for many years over this and pray that one day we can have a relationship again, but for now, I accept that she doesn't want me in her life. I would be lying if I said this doesn't rip me in half, but I can try to help others, so they don't have to experience it.

My eldest daughter and I do have a relationship, and I am grateful for that every day.

My parents

I made my amends to my mum and dad face to face, and they forgave all of the pain I had caused and were so proud of me for finally getting sober. I put them through years of pain and uncertainty, and I am truly grateful for their love and their care of both myself and the girls for all of those missing years.

My ex-husbands

I made amends to both. In AA, there is a saying, "Keep your side of the street clean," and I did that. The relationships were not perfect, and I can't have been easy to live with; untreated alcoholism is ugly.

Shaun

That man has been my rock for so many years, even though he never judged me on and off. Shaun knew that I had a problem and was in emotional pain long before I ever did. I made my amends, and we can laugh about some of my antics these days. We also talk about our baby that never got to be, and again, I write these so others can hopefully learn that they or a loved one can get off the drink rollercoaster at any time, and I hope sooner rather than later.

The "Promises" of Recovery

Throughout my amends process, S told me about the promises of recovery, and this kept me going, especially when some of my amends were met with hostility. This was to be expected as I had been highly thoughtless. They say hurt people hurt people, and this was true for me.

These promises include freedom from the obsession with alcohol, a newfound sense of peace, improved relationships, and a general feeling of well-being. Alcoholics find that their outlook on life changes, and they gain the ability to handle challenges that once seemed overwhelming.

Some of the key promises mentioned include:

- A sense of freedom and happiness.

- No longer regretting the past or wishing to shut the door on it.
- A newfound peace and serenity, regardless of life's external circumstances.

These promises have turned out to be accurate, and I promise you that it works. It was worth every ounce of pain to get to this.

I tried everything to stop drinking, and nothing worked. I am now a free woman, and although I can't change the past, it has made me a strong woman, not a victim. I get to help others achieve sobriety daily, which is a gift.

The past took some getting rid of as I felt guilty over my children to the point of depression, and sometimes I still do.

What do I do with this?

I talk about it.

These days, I have many wonderful friends, and a unique spiritual sister called Sandra, who has helped me so much over the last few years. I am forever grateful. I don't bottle up my feelings; I let them out and talk about them. Alcoholics think slightly differently from ordinary people and can become stuck in themselves with ease, and sometimes, I need someone to say stop it. I did the best I could do at the time.

In my six years of sobriety, life has given me many knocks, such as an autoimmune disorder, deaths of friends and family ill health, and I have been able to deal with this without a drink; the big point to make here is a drink would have made it worse.

These days, I can enjoy life on life's terms, and life is never easy, but it's previous, and I deserve to live it.

Step 10: Continuing Personal Inventory

Step 10. We continued to take personal inventory and, when we were wrong, promptly admitted it.

Getting to this point in my recovery had taken a few weeks, and this is how I work with new ladies who want recovery as freely as it was given to me.

I had a little get-together at my house with some sober ladies to share experiences of how they work in step 1 and incorporate this into their daily lives.

Step 10 calls for alcoholics to continue to take personal inventory regularly and promptly admit when they are wrong. This step is about maintaining the progress made through the previous steps by staying vigilant and self-aware. Alcoholics are encouraged to watch for selfishness, dishonesty, resentment, and fear and to address these issues as they arise rather than letting them fester.

In early sobriety, I regularly took personal inventory as I had to. I had been a badass for so long I was learning how to become a good person with morals. Some people say we alcoholics stop maturing the day we took our first drink, and for me, that was early days, which made me around 7 and 3 quarters.

These days, I'm around 18, so it's still a work in progress. I apologize when needed and commonly know right away when I have been an ass.

My big takeaway is to keep my ego in check and not become the centre of the universe yet again. It's not extensive or clever, and it's exhausting. I had to remain humble and live in the present moment and not worry about everything and every possible outcome as I wasn't in charge anymore (not that I ever really was)

Step 11: Seeking Spiritual Growth

Step 11. Through prayer and meditation, we sought to improve our conscious contact with God as we understood him, praying only for his knowledge, his will for us, and the power to carry that out.

Prayer and Meditation

Step 11 encourages alcoholics to improve their conscious contact with a higher power through prayer and meditation. The focus is on seeking knowledge of a higher power's will and gaining the strength to carry it out. This step is about deepening the spiritual connection introduced in earlier steps.

I believe that we all work on the AA in our own way.

I will never be complacent as alcohol remains a cunning foe, and whenever I am sober, it's in the background doing pushes, ready to take me down.

In early sobriety, I was super conscientious and always looking to be a spiritual goddess and would nail myself to the cross whenever I messed up.

Today, I feel comfortable in my skin and accept that I don't always get things right, but I believe that as long as I'm trying my best and remain teachable, I won't go far wrong.

I am always willing to change, and when something gets to me, I ask myself if there is truth in it and, if so, what I can do. If not, and it's just someone being hurtful, then it's ok, as I don't have to take their views on board.

I can now make amends when needed, and I don't have to sit ruminating on things forever, and this is so refreshing.

I can be self-reflective these days without being in my diamond-encrusted pity pot. I try to live a spiritually cantered life without complacency and with gratitude, as even my worst day sober is better than my best day drinking.

Another Anthony DeMello comment, "I'm an ass, you're an ass; what do you expect from an ass."

Today, I can laugh at myself, and most of all, I don't take myself too seriously; life is short, and I am funny.

I pray and meditate, and it's not a chore or an emergency service. I pray and talk to God like he is my best mate and dad as, after all, he is my Abba Father.

The emphasis is on continuous self-improvement, ongoing connection with a higher power, and living a life of service and humility.

Getting sober is one thing and very commendable, but emotional sobriety is the goal. I have an excellent relationship with my higher power these days. The god of my understanding supports me with patience, love, and understanding in every aspect of my life.

He has to be patient, as it's me.

Step 12. Working with others

Having had a spiritual awakening as the result of these steps, we tried to carry the message to alcoholics and to practice these principles in all our affairs.

I am ashamed that I thought I wouldn't want to do this, but this is the most rewarding part of my life. I can pass on the message of recovery to the next suffering alcoholic, and I cannot explain enough the joy it gives me to see the light come back on in someone's eyes who has lost all hope.
I can use all of my past experiences to help the next suffering alcoholic.
They say that nothing is wasted on God's earth, and he will turn every experience, good and bad, to help another one of his kids. All I have to do is fetch wood and carry water to continue living as a free woman.
Pretty good going for an old lush, eh?

My life today and my mission of hope. Top of Form

I can say hand on heart that if anyone had told me ten years ago that I would be six and a half years sober and happy, I would have laughed in their face. I would also probably have said something sarcastic and nasty.

My journey hasn't been easy, and neither has my life.

I know some people have beautiful lives and seem to float through life. They get married once and have children, have great holidays, and enjoy a glass of wine now and again without it ever becoming a problem.

I used to be jealous to death of those people. I would watch them have a glass of wine and sometimes even leave most of it as it wasn't to their taste. I would have drunk it on the opposite end of the scale, even if a wasp was floating in it. I would have bravely taken my chances and wouldn't say I like wasps.

I remember my first AA meeting thirteen years ago when I thought I was so much better than others in the meeting. I heard a man say I am a grateful alcoholic, and I thought, what a nob, fancy saying that when he is doomed never to have a drink again.

I am Mandy, and I am a grateful, recovered alcoholic.

What I mean by that is that I no longer obsess over drinking, not one bit.

I remember that day this happened, and it struck me watching a movie at home, and I thought, OMG, I haven't thought about drinking all day, and more importantly, I haven't thought about not drinking all day.

For years, if I ever had a short period of painful abstinence, every thought was, I'm not drinking today; shoot me now.

I have recovered from the obsession with drinking. I am careful because I don't want to relapse on a risotto, champagne truffle, or mouthwash.

I would never want that awful rollercoaster to begin again. It has been a hell of a journey, and I can't return to the starting blocks.

Today, I still attend AA meetings, not because I have to but because I want to. I want and need to bring this message to the next suffering alcoholic, as it was freely given to me.

I pray daily, and as prayer is a conversation, I listen, although not always.

I am no saint and get things wrong daily, sometimes hourly, but today, I accept myself and love myself for the woman I am.

I believe nothing is wasted in God's world, and all of my trauma and pain have made me into who I am today. Without my experiences, I wouldn't be able to help others.

I feel blessed and grateful that I am alive today and that I no longer exist and waste the life I live.

To the reader, if you have an addiction or have a loved one who you are watching bring their life to the ground, know there is a great deal of hope.

We do recover, and if I can, anyone can do it regardless of circumstances.

Admitting to a problem is the first step, and submission is vital to life and future happiness.

You got this, and I believe in you as a fellow brother or sister.

Take this as a sign of hope, love, and life.

Thank you for reading my book, and I hope you got something from it.

Printed in Great Britain
by Amazon